VICTORY BEER
RECIPES

VICTORY BEER RECIPES
AMERICA'S BEST HOMEBREWS

Compiled by the
American Homebrewers Association
James Spence, Managing Editor

 Brewers Publications, Boulder, Colorado USA

Victory Beer Recipes
Managing Editor: James L. Spence
Copy Editor: Dena Nishek
Technical Editor: Philip W. Fleming
Copyright © 1994 by the Association of Brewers Inc.

ISBN 0-937381-41-1
Printed in the United States of America
10 9 8 7 6 5 4 3 2

Complied by the American Homebrewers Association

Cover Design: Vicki Hopewell
Cover Illustration: Dan Hatala
Interior Design: Wendy Rodgers/Susie Marcus
Brewing Photographers: Marilyn Cohen, Elizabeth Gold,
                Vicki Hopewell
Brewing Models: Sarah Chesnutt, Marilyn Cohen, Elizabeth Gold
                Vicki Hopewell, Matt Morton, Bill Simpson
Interior Illustrations Art: John Martin
Judging Photographer: Karen Barela at the 1994 AHA National
                Homebrew Competition judging
Published by Brewers Publications Inc., a division of the
Association of Brewers Inc., PO Box 1679, Boulder CO 80306-
1679 USA, (303) 447-0816; FAX: (303) 447-2825.

CONTENTS

DEDICATION

You are one of many people in the world who love fresh homebrew — your homebrew. The one you brewed one weekend, coaxed carefully through fermentation, then bottled, aged patiently, and popped opened one day for that first taste. No matter how good a brewer you are, no matter how careful or meticulous, that first taste is always exciting. Exciting because no one else in the world has had this beer before. You made it. It's yours. This book is for you.

We'd like to thank the homebrewers and sponsors of the American Homebrewers Association National Homebrew Competitions. Their enthusiastic participation and support for fifteen years of competition has made the hobby of homebrewing fun, exciting, and educational for tens of thousands of people around the world. This book contains winning recipes from the past five years: 1989 through 1993.

FOREWORD

BY PETE SLOSBERG

Victory Beer Recipes, America's Best Homebrew caused me to flash back to 1979, the year President Carter legalized homebrewing. This was the year I started homebrewing. Back in the late 1970s, the variety of generally available beers was extremely limited, and my taste for 99 percent of them was non-existent. Basic homebrewing equipment, supplies, and recipes were available, so my experimentation began.

What I really could have used in the beginning was a book that went into detail with descriptions and recipes for a wide range of styles.

Victory Beer Recipes takes homebrewing to the next level! Not only does this book list an extremely wide variety of styles with detailed recipes and procedures, these are award-winning formulas! In my experience as a Certified Beer Judge Certification Program judge, I've judged hundreds of homebrews and commercial beers. Only a small handful of those are worthy of being called world-class beers. This book, however, contains details on world-class beers.

I had the pleasure of judging one of these beers and tasting another. Paddy Giffen's "Kilts on Fire" Smoked Scottish Wee Heavy won first place in the Smoked Beer category and then went on to win Best of Show in 1993 at the AHA National Homebrewers Competition in Portland, Ore. [Paddy was awarded Homebrewer of the year in 1993.] I rated this beer with the highest score I've ever given a beer. To my amazement the other three judges gave it similarly high marks.

I also tasted Ron Page's Chocolate Chambord Stout. This beer, which came in first in the Specialty Beer category in 1993, was an incredible sensory experience with bold raspberry and chocolate taste and aroma that added an extra dimension.

The next best thing to drinking these truly incredible world-class beers is having their formulas to work with at home. This book brings it all together with the background on the styles, recipes, judges comments, and then the names and addresses of the brewers.

If only I had this book 15 years ago!

Pete Slosberg is the founder of fifth largest specialty brewing company in the United States – Pete's Brewing Company. His well-known Pete's Wicked Ale began as a homebrewing experiment and evolved from Pete's philosophy:"Take the beer seriously, but have fun doing it!"

He still homebrews in his kitchen on weekends and travels extensively around the world tasting different beers. Pete's Brewing Company was recognized by Inc. *magazine October 1993 as the thirty-third fastest growing private company in the United States.*

INTRODUCTION

Do you know what makes a truly great homebrew? Just the simple fact that you brewed it. If you can make the same exact beer again, terrific, but you don't have to. In fact, lots of homebrewers have never made the same recipe more than once. There are simply too many different brews to make.

Since 1979, the American Homebrewers Association has sponsored the National Homebrew Competition. In 1993, there were 2,747 entries from around the world. The brews — beer, mead, saké, and cider — were judged at six different sites, and required more than 15,000 people-hours to receive, unpack, label, register, judge, mail results, etc. The goal of the AHA National Homebrew Competition is to encourage brewers to improve their brewing by providing feedback from accredited judges. Brewers who enter the AHA National Homebrew Competition get at least two score sheets from the judges who judged their beer. These score sheets have tasting notes, comments, and suggestions for improving the beer. It is one of the most valuable resources homebrewers have for a fun and educational homebrewing experience.

Since 1993, the Competition has been divided into twenty-eight categories, encompassing beer, mead, cider, and saké. Each category has one or more subcategories, creating a total of seventy-three different homebrew styles to be judged. In 1993, the Competition used three rounds of judging. Brewers entering the first round sent one bottle of each entry to one of six regional sites: four beer and mead sites, one site each for cider and saké. The beers and meads were judged and the

---

Victory Beer Recipes

top three finishers in each category from each site advanced to the second round, making a total of twelve brews in each category competing in the second round. Cider and saké were judged independently at their respective sites. In the second round, the twelve beers were judged, and a first, second, and third place were chosen in each category. The twenty-four first place beers advanced to the best-of-show round, where four of the country's most experienced judges picked the best beer, the brewer of which is named Homebrewer of the Year. The best mead earns its maker Meadmaker of the Year. Cidermaker of the Year and Sakémaker of the Year are also chosen in separate judgings.

How to Use This Book

Most of the information included in this book is taken from the information supplied by competitors and judges for the AHA National Homebrew Competition. The style guidelines are in constant evolution and expansion, and the American Homebrewers Association will be the last to say that the style guidelines used in the Competition are the only source to use when you brew. There are hundreds of different beer styles, and some of the world's classic beers do not fit neatly into the Competition guidelines. Our attempt is to define some of the better-known styles by providing the best and most up-to-date information we can. But it isn't gospel. We change them to accommodate suggestions from AHA members, brewers, judges, and to include styles that are newly popular. The guidelines are simply a tool, a measuring stick, to help homebrewers compare their own brews to the ones they buy or taste.

This book contains 128 recipes that won first, second, or third place in their categories in the AHA National Homebrew Competitions 1989, 1990, 1991, 1992, and 1993. As you peruse them, think of them as your own. Keep in mind that your results may vary. Each recipe is taken directly from the brewer's recipe form (Farhenheit and Celsius temperatures have been rounded to the nearest half-degree.) We didn't brew them ourselves or test them in any way. We've included some ways for you to estimate the results you'll get before you brew, but we urge you to be creative, change the recipes here and there if you want. See what great brews you can come up with. Remember, it's your brew.

We've tried to select a broad range of recipes for this book. The idea is to give you as many choices as we can to help you brew your best. For example, we included fruit beer and herb beer recipes that we felt were creative, original, and interesting to brew and taste. One thing the recipes in this book do have in common is their winning performances in the AHA National Homebrew Competitions.

To accommodate all-extract, grain/extract, and all-grain brewers, for each style we have provided a mixture, in most cases, of brewing techniques. You can convert an all-grain recipe to extract and vice versa, and we've included some conversion guidelines in the appendix that should help .

Most of the recipes include a short section of brewer's specifics that describe any specific or unusual processes the brewer used. You should also read the judges' comments, because even winning brews sometimes need fine-tuning. The comments may let you know what areas to focus on to make the beer the best it can be.

At the beginning of each chapter is a brief background of the style, and the style guidelines used in the 1993 AHA National Homebrew Competition. During the past fifteen years, the styles have expanded and evolved to the current (1993) twenty-four categories of lager, ale, and mixed-style beers, two categories of mead, one category of cider, and one category of saké. Most categories have subcategories, resulting in a total of seventy-three different styles of homebrew judged.

A style characteristic designated "OK" means it does not have to be apparent but is acceptable in the amounts indicated. When the term "noble-type" hops is used, it refers to European continental-type hops such as Saaz, Hallertauer, Tettnanger, and Spalter, to name a few.

Each chapter introduces the beer style and presents style guidelines that provide useful brewing information including ranges for: original gravity (OG) — the specific gravity reading prior to fermentation; percent alcohol by volume — the apparent alcohol content of the beer; International Bittering Units (IBUs) — a measure of the total quantity of bittering compounds in the beer; and SRM (Standard Research Method) — a measure of how much light is transmitted by a beer and is how beer color is measured. Keep in mind that SRM is a measure of how translucent or opaque a beer is, not the actual color our eyes perceive. Two beers with the same SRM can actually be different in color. For example, one could be light brown, the other deep golden. Lovibond degrees (°L) is an older color measurement system similar to the SRM sytem.

That's pretty much all you need to know to make good use of this classic collection of recipes. Let's cut the shuck and jive and get on with the recipes!

PART I

ALE

Ales are distinguished by the use of top-fermenting *Saccharomyces cerevisiae* yeast strains. These strains perform at warmer temperatures, the ferments are faster and fermentation by-products are generally more evident. Ales tend to have a very pronounced palate where esters and fruity qualities are part of the character.

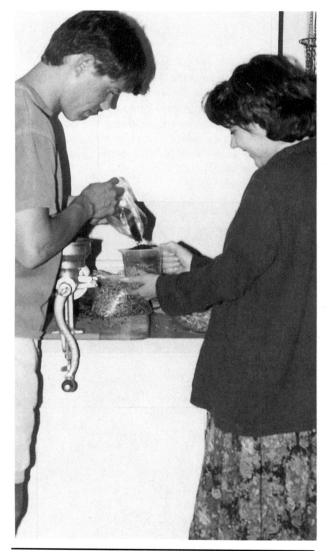

CHAPTER 1

BARLEY WINE

Barley wines are famous for their considerable malt character plus high hopping rate to balance the malty sweetness. Commercial examples of this style in America tend to be quite hoppy in flavor, while English examples are maltier in character. The high original gravity of this style makes it ideal for long-term aging, in some cases for several years. A strong flavor of alcohol, and a deep, rich fruitiness should be prevalent. Homebrewers sometimes use Champagne or wine yeast to ferment these beers, although it is not necessary to do so in all cases. Use a good and large yeast starter, and be prepared to wait a little while for your barley wine to ferment and age.

AHA National Homebrew Competition Style Guidelines
Copper to medium brown. Malty sweetness. Fruity/estery. Medium to high body. Medium to high bitterness. Hop aroma and flavor OK. Alcoholic taste. Low to medium diacetyl OK.

OG (Balling/Plato)	Percent alc./vol.	IBUs	SRM
1.090-1.120 (22.5-30)	8.4-12%	50-100	14-22

WILLY'S BEST

Barley Wine
First Place, Barley Wine, 1989
Clay Biberdorf, St. Charles, Missouri
(grain/extract)

Ingredients for 5 gallons

11	pounds pale ale malt
4	pounds Alexander's Sun Country malt extract
3	pounds light dry malt extract
1/2	pound crystal malt
1/2	pound Munich malt
2	ounces Eroica hops (60 minutes)
2	ounces Galena hops (40 minutes)
1	ounce Hallertauer hops (five minutes)
1	ounce Hallertauer hops (dry hop)
1	ounce Tettnanger hops (dry hop)
1	ounce East Kent Golding hops, (dry hop)
	Brewer's Choice liquid ale yeast
	Montrachet Champagne yeast

Original specific gravity: 1.103
Final specific gravity: 1.030
Boiling time: 60 minutes
Primary fermentation: seven days at 66 degrees F (19 degrees C) in glass
Secondary fermentation: three weeks
Age when judged (since bottling): 14 months

Judges' comments

"Fruity, estery aroma, more hops than malt at first — then malty. Light brown color, hazy, great head retention. Good malt-bitterness balance. Malty, bitter finish; smooth. A good beer although not as complex as some."

"Malty nose. Head fell quickly, but nice pinpoint carbonation. Flavor has a good malty start and the hops come through in the finish. Could be a little thicker."

"Hop, malt, and slight sour aroma, old hops? Appearance is tawny, hazy, OK. Sweet malty flavor with a big hop bite! Overall a big full flavor, good recipe; something is slightly off. Try to be cleaner."

FOGHORN LEGHORN BARLEYWINE

Barley Wine
First Place, Barley Wine, 1992
Greg Leas, St. Charles, Missouri
(grain/extract)

Ingredients for 5 gallons

10	pounds two-row malt
4	pounds pale malt
1	pound 40 °L crystal malt
1	pound CaraPils malt
3.3	pounds Northwestern malt extract
4	pounds Alexander malt extract
3	ounces Centennial hops, 9.1 percent alpha acid (60 minutes)
1	ounce Northern Brewer hops, 6.7 percent alpha acid (60 minutes)
1	ounce East Kent Goldings hops, alpha acid 5.3 percent (one minute)
	Wyeast No. 1056 liquid yeast

Original specific gravity: 1.096
Final specific gravity: 1.025
Boiling time: 60 minutes
Primary fermentation: 14 days at 70 degrees F (21 degrees C) in glass
Secondary fermentation: 14 days at 70 degrees F (21 degrees C) in glass
Age when judged (since bottling): 12 months

Brewer's specifics

Mash grains for 90 minutes at 153 degrees F (67 degrees C) until conversion.

Judges' comments

"A nice brew. Malty, hop bitterness appropriate. Alcohol evident. Color at light end of spectrum."
"Nice hop-malt balance."
"Very good barley wine. Very sweet, malty nose. Spicy aroma. Not enough fruitiness — perhaps try a different yeast. Nice job."
"Great beer, clean, well-made."

Bip Bam Hot Damn

Barley Wine
Second Place, Barley Wine, 1990
Norman Dickenson, Santa Rosa, California
(grain/extract)

Ingredients for 5 gallons

11	pounds two-row Klages malt
5	pounds light dry malt extract
2	pounds Munich malt
12	ounces dark molasses
2 3/4	ounces chocolate malt
1	ounce Nugget hops (60 minutes)
3/4	ounce Cluster hops (60 minutes)
1	ounce Nugget hops (35 minutes)
1/2	ounce Styrian Goldings hops (35 minutes)
3/4	ounce Styrian Goldings hops (20 minutes)
1/2	ounce Cascade hops (10 minutes)
1/2	ounce Styrian Goldings hops (10 minutes)
1/2	ounce Hallertauer hops (dry hop)
3	teaspoons gypsum
1/4	teaspoon Epsom salts
	Red Star dry Champagne yeast
1 1/2	cups corn sugar to prime

Original specific gravity: 1.093
Final specific gravity: 1.034
Boiling time: 60 minutes
Primary fermentation: eight days at 57 degrees F (14 degrees C) in glass
Secondary fermentation: 14 days at 57 degrees F (14 degrees C) in glass
Age when judged (since bottling): four months

Brewer's specifics

Mash grains at 156 degrees F (69 degrees C) for 60 minutes.

Judges' comments

"Sweet malty aroma with just a touch of dark roast grain. Full body. Big, nay, huge! Big, malty clean and very drinkable. A winner."
"Good beer overall. Nice brewing. More hop aroma and some malt body needed. Very well made."
"Very nice looking beer. Too sweet, not enough hops for balance."

ROBERT THE BRUCE

Barley Wine
Second Place, Barley Wine, 1992
Rob Brunner, Windsor, Colorado
(grain/extract)

Ingredients for 5 gallons

12	pounds Wander light malt extract
4	pounds pale ale malt
1	pound 20 °L crystal malt
2	ounces British Bold hops, 10 percent alpha acid (45 minutes)
1 1/2	ounces Centennial hops, 7.5 percent alpha acid (45 minutes)
2	ounces Kent Goldings hops, 5.9 percent alpha acid (finish)
1	ounce Kent Goldings hops, 4.8 percent alpha acid (finish)
	Wyeast No. 1084 Irish ale yeast
	Vierka Champagne yeast
3/4	cup dextrose to prime

Original specific gravity: 1.110
Final specific gravity: 1.034
Primary Fermentation: 10 days at 72 degrees F (22 degrees C) in glass
Secondary Fermentation: 21 days at 60 degrees F (15.5 degrees C) in oak
Age when judged (since bottling): 16 months

Judges' comments

"Overconditioned. Pleasant alcoholic warmness. A very nice beer."
"Right on target. Nice color."
"Hop flavor and bitterness dominate. Some malty sweetness. Alcoholic. Higher alcohols evident — somewhat solventlike. Good beer, not much fine tuning needed here."
"Clean brew. Seems a bit thin for style. A bit more malt could have lessened higher alcohols and given more body."

BOOBS BARLEY WINE

Barley Wine
Second Place, Barley Wine, 1993
Chuck Boyce, Cincinnati, Ohio
(grain/extract)

Ingredients for 5 gallons

12	pounds light malt extract
3	pounds Klages malt
1/2	pound dextrin malt
1/2	pound crystal malt
9	ounces Bullion hops (90 minutes)
1 1/2	ounces Fuggles hops (15 minutes)
1 1/2	ounces Cascade hops (one to two minutes)
	Wyeast No. 1056 liquid yeast culture
3/4	cup corn sugar to prime

Original specific gravity: 1.110
Final specific gravity: 1.034
Boiling time: 90 minutes
Primary fermentation: four weeks at 75 degrees F (24 degrees C) in glass
Secondary fermentation: two weeks at 65 degrees F (18 degrees C) in glass
Age when judged (since bottling): 14 months

Brewer's specifics

Mash grains for one hour at 152 degrees F (67 degrees C).

Judges' comments

"Very well done. Lots of hops in aroma and flavor which follows through. Nothing odd detected. Seems very clean, but lacks complexity. Body may be on the light side."
"Rather bitter. A bit more unfermentables, please."
"Very malty, rich and hoppy. Nice drinkable brew."
"Slightly overhopped. Good body, could take a little more. Very smooth."
"Good flavor, but lacks intensity. Seems soft, finish a bit harsh. Medium body needs a bit more stuffing."

CHAPTER 2

BELGIAN-STYLE SPECIALTY

The beers of Belgium are some of the most unusual and varied in the world. From the more typical pale ale style to the mysterious lambic, Belgian beers will really test your brewing skills. Belgian brewers use, along with other standard ingredients, unique yeast strains, unmalted wheat, candi sugar, and non-standard fermentation temperatures. Lambic-style beers are pitched by opening the windows or vents of the brewery at night allowing wild yeast and bacteria to inoculate the wort — the process that produces the classic sourness inherent in these beers. To get the best results, pick a suitable yeast strain, and try to use ingredients and procedures that model those of the Belgian breweries.

AHA National Homebrew Competition Style Guidelines

a) Flanders Brown – Slight sourness and spiciness. Deep copper to brown. Fruity/estery. No hop flavor or aroma. Low to medium bitterness. Low diacetyl OK.

b) Dubbel – Dark amber to brown. Sweet malty, nutty aroma. Faint hop aroma OK. Medium to full body. Low bitterness. Low diacetyl OK.

c) Trippel – Light/pale color. Light malty and hop aroma. Neutral hop/malt balance. Finish may be sweet. Medium to full body. Alcoholic, but best examples do not taste strongly of alcohol.

d) Belgian Ale – Pale color. A Belgian "pale ale." Bitterness subdued. Light to medium body. Low malt aroma. Slight acidity OK. Low diacetyl OK.

e) Belgian Strong Ale – Pale to dark brown. Alcoholic. Can be vinous. Darker beers are colored with candi sugar and not much dark malt. Full body.

f) Lambic-style – Intensely and cleanly sour. No hop bitterness, flavor or aroma. Effervescent. Fruity/estery and uniquely aromatic. Malted barley and unmalted wheat. Stale, old hops used. Cloudiness OK. Types:

Faro – Lambic with sugar and sometimes caramel added. Pale to light amber.

Gueuze – Unflavored lambic. Pale. Often very dry. Diacetyl very low.

Fruit (Framboise, Kriek, Peche) – Raspberry, cherry, peach, etc., fermented and flavored lambic. Fruit flavor, aroma, and color are intense. Sourness predominates. Often very dry.

g) White – Unmalted wheat and malted barley. Oats OK. Usually spiced with coriander seed and orange peel. Noble-type hop flavor and aroma desired. Low to medium bitterness. Low to medium body. Dry. Low diacetyl OK. Low to medium esters.

OG (Balling/Plato)	Percent alc./vol.	IBUs	SRM
a) Flanders Brown			
1.045-56 (11-14)	4.8-5.2%	15-25	10-20
b) Dubbel			
1.050-70 (12.5-17.5)	6-7.5%	18-25	10-14
c) Trippel			
1.070-95 (17.5-24)	7-10%	20-25	3.5-5.5
d) Belgian Ale			
1.044-54 (11-13.5)	4-6%	20-30	3.5-12
e) Belgian Strong Ale			
1.063-95 (16-24)	7-12%	20-50	3.5-20
f) Lambic-style: Faro			
1.044-56 (11-14)	5-6%	11-13	6-15
Gueuze			
1.044-56 (11-14)	5-6%	11-13	6-13
Fruit (Framboise, Kriek, Pêche)			
1.040-72 (10-17.5)	5-7%	15-21	—
g) White			
1.044-50 (11-12.5)	4.5-5.2%	15-25	2-4

IT IS WALLOON

Saison
Second Place, Belgian-style Specialty, 1990
Philip Markowski, New Haven, Connecticut
(all grain)

Ingredients for 4 gallons

7 2/3	pounds English two-row pale malt
3 1/3	pounds malted wheat
1/2	pound Munich malt
1 1/2	ounces Saaz hops (60 minutes)
3/4	ounce Cascade hops (60 minutes)
1/4	ounce Saaz hops (five minutes)
1/4	ounce Cascade hops (five minutes)
1/4	teaspoon acid blend
	Wyeast No. 3056 wheat beer yeast
1/2	cup dried malt extract to prime

Original specific gravity: 1.048
Final specific gravity: 1.013
Boiling time: 60 minutes
Primary fermentation: two weeks at 62 degrees F (16.5 degrees C) in glass
Secondary fermentation: two weeks in glass
Age when judged (since bottling): three months

Brewer's specifics

Step infusion mash. Protein rest at 123 degrees F (50.5 degrees C) for 35 minutes. Rest at 144 degrees F (62 degrees C) for 20 minutes. Rest at 152 degrees F (66.5 degrees C) for 30 minutes. Heat to mash-out at 160 degrees F (71 degrees C), then sparge with 4 gallons 172-degree-F (78-degree-C) water.

Judges' comments

"Very nice blend of malt, hops, and sour aroma. Bright appearance. Flavor is great! Nice balance. Overall a fine effort. You did well."

"Nice grainy aroma. Nice head; slight haze. Heavily hopped — overpowers other flavors. Lacks the sourness of the saison category. Very lingering hop flavor."

"Smells like a good cream ale; nice hops; touch of DMS. Very clean and creamy with outstanding malt to hops balance. Fresh, grainy aftertaste. Delicious, refreshing, almost lagerlike ale. Fine job!"

CREAM CITY ABBEY ALE

Trappist Ale
Second Place, Belgian-style Specialty, 1990
Robert Burko, Milwaukee, Wisconsin
(all grain)

Ingredients for 5 gallons

7	pounds two-row malt
3	pounds Munich malt
3/4	ounce chocolate malt
1/2	pound brown sugar
5	ounces molasses
1 1/2	ounces Saaz hops (60 minutes)
1/2	ounce Willamette hops (one minute)
	Chimay liquid yeast culture
3/4	cup dextrose to prime

Original specific gravity: 1.063
Final specific gravity: 1.015
Boiling time: 60 minutes
Primary fermentation: 14 days at 68 degrees F (20 degrees C) in glass
Age when judged (since bottling): five months

Brewer's specifics

Mash-in with 13 quarts of 135-degree-F (57-degree-C) water. Rest one-half hour at 124 degrees F (51 degrees C). Mash grains for one hour at 155 degrees F (68 degrees C), then raise to 168 degrees F (75.5 degrees C) for five minutes. Sparge with 5 1/2 gallons of pH 5.7 water at 168 degrees F (75.5 degrees C).

Judges' comments

"Malty/phenolic aroma — appropriate for style. Phenolic taste up front and dry finish. Middle of the road body — like a Chimay. Well done. I like this one."

"Malty/fruit balance very nice in aroma. A hint of spice. Nice color, a bit cloudy but that's normal. Nice balance in taste. Clove and fruit show but don't overpower. Very nice beer — reminds me of a Chimay Red. Good effort."

"Really wonderful typically Belgian style. Not too alcoholic. Great balance between esters and subtle, delicate lactic sourness."

DUBBEL QUEENSBERRY FRAMBOISE

Trappist Ale
First Place, Belgian-style Specialty, 1989
Paul Prozeller, Hamden, Connecticut
1989 Homebrewer of the Year
(all grain)

Ingredients for 5 gallons

6 1/2	pounds two-row pale ale malt
2	pounds wheat malt
1	ounce Fuggles hops (60 minutes)
1/3	ounce Challenger hops (20 minutes)
11	pints raspberries
1	teaspoon gypsum
	Williams' liquid German alt yeast

Original specific gravity: 1.055
Final specific gravity: 1.009
Boiling time: 60 minutes
Primary fermentation: three to four weeks at 70 degrees F (21 degrees C) in stainless steel
Secondary fermentation: yes
Age when judged (since bottling): two months

Brewer's specifics

Half-hour protein rest at 120 degrees F (49 degrees C). One-hour saccharification rest at 155 degrees F (68.5 degrees C). Boil one hour. Prime using one quart 1.052-gravity wort.

Judges' comments

"Appropriate aroma. Beautiful color. Excellent beer — nice and tart. Totally appropriate for style."
"Powerful raspberry aroma followed by dirty, wet-stone nuttiness. Lovely salmon-pink color. Cloudiness not inappropriate to style. Great berry tartness on entry, but wild yeast expressed more as dirtiness than sourness. Interested to know what yeast you used. Perhaps some experimenting with yeast would help, but fine job overall."
"Raspberry-grainy aroma. Slight haze; beautiful color. A nice raspberry blended flavor; nice lingering aftertaste. Good overall."

JACKIE'S ABBEY

Trappist Ale
Second Place, Belgian-style Specialty, 1991
Jackie Keith, Louisville, Kentucky
(grain/extract)

Ingredients for 5 gallons

12	pounds Alexander's pale malt extract
6	ounces crystal malt
4	ounces chocolate malt
1 3/4	ounces Bullion hops, 9 percent alpha acid (45 minutes)
1/4	ounce Perle hops, 7.4 percent alpha acid (45 minutes)
1	teaspoon Irish moss (15 minutes)
3/4	ounce Saaz hops, 4.4 percent alpha acid (10 minutes)
3/4	ounce Hallertauer hops, 3 percent alpha acid (10 minutes)
1/4	ounce Saaz hops, 4.4 percent alpha acid (one minute)
1/4	ounce Hallertauer hops, 3 percent alpha acid (one minute)
	Cultured Chimay yeast
3/4	cup corn sugar to prime

Original specific gravity: 1.068
Final specific gravity: 1.018
Boiling time: 60 minutes
Primary fermentation: 15 days at 65 degrees F (18 degrees C) in glass
Age when judged (since bottling): two months

Brewer's specifics

Pre-boil filtered water for one hour. Steep grains at 175 degrees F (79 degrees C).

Judges' comments

"A super-fine beer. Just a little dark and toasty for a trippel. Excellent."
"This beer straddles the subcategories. Well-made, but a bit simple. Try a yeast that adds more character."
"Good drinkability with nutty character. English hop character. Taste of a dubbel, alcohol of a trippel."

TRAPPIST ALE

Trappist Ale
First Place, Belgian-style Specialty, 1990
Terry Olesen, St. Charles, Missouri
(grain/extract)

Ingredients for 5 gallons

6	pounds Edme light dry malt extract
2	pounds Munich malt
2 1/2	pounds orange blossom honey
1/2	pound wheat malt
2	ounces black patent malt
1	ounce Hallertauer hops (35 minutes)
1	ounce Hallertauer hops (25 minutes)
1	ounce Hallertauer hops (15 minutes)
1	ounce Hallertauer hops (10 minutes)
1/2	ounce Fuggles hop pellets (dry hop)
	Cultured Chimay yeast

Original specific gravity: 1.074
Final specific gravity: 1.012
Primary fermentation: four days at 60 degrees F (15.5 degrees C) in glass
Secondary fermentation: eight days at 60 degrees F (15.5 degrees C) in glass
Tertiary fermentation: five months at 40 degrees F (4.5 degrees C) in stainless-steel keg
Age when judged (since bottling): two months

Brewer's specifics

Pre-boil all water. Mash for 30 minutes at 130 degrees F (54.5 degrees C). Bring to 150 degrees F (65.5 degrees C) for 90 minutes. Raise to 168 degrees F (75.5 degrees C) for 10 minutes. Sparge with 160-degree-F (71-degree-C) water. Force carbonated.

Judges' comments

"Trappist yeast-phenolic nose very appropriate! Dry and phenolic warming in the finish. Could use a bit more malt body for balance of a wonderful beer. Great beer. Good job. Mash at a slightly higher temperature to create more limited dextrins and you'll have the perfect Trappist Chimay."

"Buttery, caramel nose. Good malt and some hops in aroma. Excellent appearance, pretty beer. Good malt sweetness, balanced. Some lactic taste; good hop bitterness. Very good body. Right amount of alcohol. Slightly phenolic, but to style. Tart, refreshing finish. Good try."

"Spicy aroma. Very clear appearance, nice color. Nice malt and traditional spice flavor. Alcohol and hops make a long, warm finish. Body is just about right. Overall a very fine effort."

"Really nice fruity aroma, estery nose. Subtle, rich, malty and complex. Excellent appearance. Body is almost a camel-hair shirt, hardwood-pewed, genuflecting Trappist ale. Overall, I think I saw God."

SHE WILL

Trappist Ale
First Place, Belgian-style Specialty, 1991
Mark Richmond, Springfield, Ohio
(grain/extract)

Ingredients for 5 gallons

2	pounds two-row malt
1/2	pound Munich malt
1/2	pound wheat malt
3	ounces Hallertauer hops, 4 percent alpha acid (60 minutes)
1	ounce Tettnanger hops, 3.8 percent alpha acid (60 minutes)
8	pounds Munton and Fison light dry malt extract (60 minutes)
7	ounces candi sugar (60 minutes)
1	ounce Saaz hops, 3 percent alpha acid (30 minutes)
1/2	ounce Centennial hops, 12 percent alpha acid (two minutes)
	Cultured Chimay yeast in a one-quart starter
3/4	cup corn sugar to prime

Original specific gravity: 1.084
Final specific gravity: not given
Boiling time: 90 minutes
Primary fermentation: 17 days at 60 degrees F (15.5 degrees C) in glass
Age when judged (since bottling): four months

Brewer's specifics

Pre-boil all water. Step infusion mash: hold grains in protein rest at 120 degrees F (49 degrees C) for 30 minutes. Raise temperature to 140 degrees F (60 degrees C) and hold 10 minutes. Raise temperature to 158 degrees F (70 degrees C), hold 90 minutes and sparge with 165-degree-F (74-degree-C) water. Add candi sugar and malt extract 30 minutes into the 90-minute boil.

Judges' comments

"Estery, malty character in aroma. Alcohol in background, some diacetyl. Strongly alcoholic, very sweet up front. Hops a bit assertive, some astringency. Very rich body. Interesting beer, with a good fit for the trippel style. Needs a little tuning (or maybe a year's aging)."

"Spicy, citrus aroma. Some 'root beer' esters — not unpleasant. Very drinkable, has appropriate residual sweetness with good hop balance."

"Clean, powerful taste. Perfect balance! Nice lingering aftertaste. An exceptionally fine beer. True to style, very refined. Don't change anything!"

ESTER THE MOLESTER

Belgian Strong Ale
First Place, Belgian-style Specialty, 1993
Brian Bliss, Dallas, Texas
(all grain)

Ingredients for 5 gallons

9	pounds 3 °L pale ale malt
1/2	pound 77 °L CaraMunich malt
1/2	pound 25 °L aromatic malt
1/4	pound Special "B" malt
2	pounds Turbinado sugar
3 1/3	pounds amber extract
2	pounds amber dry extract
1 1/3	pounds light dry extract
3/5	pound corn sugar
3	ounces Goldings hop plugs, 5.2 percent alpha acid (70 minutes)
2	ounces Fuggles hop plugs, 4.2 percent alpha acid (70 minutes)
1	ounce Northern Brewer hop plugs, 7.5 percent alpha acid (70 minutes)
1/2	ounce Hallertauer hops, 4.5 percent alpha acid (70 minutes)
1/2	ounce Saaz hops (dry)
	Whitbread ale yeast
85	grams corn sugar (to prime in keg)
1	tablespoon black treacle (to prime in keg)

Original specific gravity: 1.100
Final specific gravity: 1.029
Boiling time: 120 minutes
Primary fermentation: six weeks at 60 to 65 degrees F (16 to 18 degrees C) in glass
Age when judged (since bottling): five months

Brewer's specifics

Mash grains at 152 degrees F (67 degrees C) for 45 minutes. Wrap fermenter in an electric blanket and heat to between 90 and 100 degrees F (32 and 38 degrees C) for 12 hours after fermentation begins.

Judges' comments

"Interesting beer with a lot going on. Alcohol is there but well-balanced with other characteristics to keep it from being too assertive. A bold brew."
"Big malt flavor, some vinousness. Lots of alcohol. Big, chewy, complex. Finishes rather quickly and pleasantly. A beautiful beer!"
"Well-balanced. Lacks some mature vinous character. A little dry in finish. Could be fuller in flavor all around. Needs to be fuller to deal with yeast attenuation."
"Nice, balanced. Rich malt tones. Black currant character."
"Sweet, noticeably alcoholic strong ale with a winy-sharp character in the flavor; long-lasting malty finish."

CHAPTER 3

BROWN ALE

English brown and mild ales are relatively malty with just a small degree of hop character. English mild has a low alcohol level suited for session drinking in the working-class pubs of western England. English browns are also relatively low in gravity. Their substantial malt character is derived from the low hopping rate and the soft water that is traditional for brewing English browns. The low gravity of these beers prevents their malt character from becoming cloying. American brown is similar to English brown, except it is typically highly hopped with North American varieties. The low gravity of brown ales results in quick fermentations. Carbonation levels are traditionally lower than other beer styles.

AHA National Homebrew Competition Style Guidelines
a) **English Brown** – Medium to dark brown. Sweet and malty. Low bitterness. Hop flavor and aroma low. Some fruitiness and esters. Medium body. Low diacetyl OK.
b) **English Mild** – Low alcohol. Medium to very dark brown. Low hop bitterness, flavor, and aroma. Mild maltiness. Light body. Low esters.
c) **American Brown** – Medium to dark brown. High hop bitterness, flavor, and aroma. Medium maltiness and body. Low diacetyl OK.

OG (Balling/Plato)	Percent alc./vol.	IBUs	SRM
a) English Brown			
1.040-50 (10-12.5)	4-5.5%	15-25	15-22
b) English Mild			
1.032-36 (8-9)	2.5-3.6%	14-20	17-34
c) American Brown			
1.040-55 (10-14)	4-5.5%	25-60	15-22

ARTHER PITHICUS BROWN

Brown Ale
First Place, Brown Ale, 1991
Kevin Johnson, Pacifica, California
(grain/extract)

Ingredients for 6 1/2 gallons

5	pounds English two-row malt
4	pounds English mild two-row malt
2	pounds English crystal malt
1 2/3	pounds John Bull amber unhopped malt extract
1/4	pound chocolate malt
1	ounce Northern Brewer hops, 7 percent alpha acid (75 minutes)
1/2	ounce Northern Brewer hops (35 minutes)
1/2	ounce Goldings hops (35 minutes)
1 1/4	ounces Goldings hops (finish)
3/4	teaspooon gypsum (half in mash, half in sparge)
	Wyeast No. 1056 Chico liquid ale yeast
3/4	cup corn sugar to prime

Original specific gravity: 1.062
Final specific gravity: 1.021
Boiling time: 75 minutes
Age when judged (since bottling): 2 1/2 months

Brewer's specifics

Mash grains at 152 to 156 degrees F (66.5 to 69 degrees C) until conversion is complete. Sparge with 170-degree-F (76.5-degree-C) water.

Judges' comments

"Super. Malt nose very evident. A little fruitiness, not much hops. Nice malt sweetness in flavor, but too gassy. Beautiful malt character with hops balanced properly. A great brown ale, but over-conditioned. Malt taste and balance are excellent."

"Malty nose with hints of grain — no hop (but that's OK for style). Good malt character throughout flavor. I like the balance of hops and malt, with malt definitely winning. When the head faded, there was a very good beer to be found. Love the malt!"

Dottie's Brown Ale

Brown Ale
Second Place, Brown Ale, 1990
Charles Lawhon, Holly Springs, North Carolina
(grain/extract)

Ingredients for 3 gallons

3 1/3	pounds American Brewmaster dark malt extract
6	ounces crystal malt
4	ounces chocolate malt
1/2	ounce Fuggles hops (60 minutes)
1/2	ounce Willamette hops (15 minutes)
1/2	ounce Willamette hops (finish)
1	teaspoon water salts
1	teaspoon Irish moss
	Wyeast No. 1084 liquid yeast in a 25-ounce starter
1/2	cup corn sugar to prime

Original specific gravity: not given
Final specific gravity: 1.012
Boiling time: 60 minutes
Primary fermentation: seven days at 70 degrees F (21 degrees C) in plastic
Age when judged (since bottling): four months

Brewer's specifics

Steep grains for 25 minutes while raising temperature from 60 degrees F (15.5 degrees C) to 212 degrees F (100 degrees C). Boil all three gallons of wort.

Judges' comments

"Good sweet aroma. Nice malt flavor and good balance. Aftertaste fades a bit quickly, and could use more malt character. Very good beer, but needs a bit more of everything to bring flavor out."
"Caramel-sweet, good low bitterness level. Aftertaste fades quickly. Body thin. A beer like Newcastle Brown Ale, but caramel character needs to be reduced. More maltiness needed."
"Boost the malt for more body and character."

SMITH 'N' HELLER

Brown Ale
First Place, Brown Ale, 1989
Thad Smith, San Francisco, California
(all grain)

Ingredients for 5 gallons

6	pounds American pale malt
5	pounds British pale malt
1	pound crystal malt
1/2	pound Munich malt
4	ounces wheat malt
1	ounce Kent Goldings hops (60 minutes)
1	ounce Kent Goldings hops (30 minutes)
2	ounces Cascade hops (eight minutes)
2	ounces Cascade hops (dry hop in secondary)
1	teaspoon salt
1/2	teaspoon gypsum
1/4	teaspoon citric acid
1/4	teaspoon Irish moss
	Wyeast No. 1056 Chico Ale liquid yeast
2/3	cup corn sugar to prime

Original specific gravity: 1.060
Final specific gravity: 1.020
Boiling time: 60 minutes
Primary fermentation: three weeks at 85 degrees F (29.5 degrees C) in glass
Secondary fermentation: one week at 85 degrees F (29.5 degrees C) in glass
Age when judged (since bottling): four months

Brewer's specifics

Step mash: 20 minutes at 110 degrees F (43.5 degrees C), 20 minutes at 125 degrees F (51.5 degrees C), 20 minutes at 135 degrees F (57 degrees C), and 20 minutes at 150 degrees F (65.5 degrees C). Base final temperature after conversion: 175 degrees F (79.5 degrees C).

Judges' comments

"Good balance in aroma; slightly hoppy. Good color and head. Good balance of flavor."

"Aroma is lacking; needs malt. Good appearance. Good balance and conditioning. Overall a nice beer!"

"Hops and malt aroma very good. Excellent color, brilliant clarity, good head retention. Very good malt flavor; very good to excellent hops; very good balance; good conditioning. Smooth, not lingering aftertaste."

SOUTHEAST TEXAS NORTHERN BROWN ALE

American Brown
Second Place, Brown Ale, 1989
Steve Daniel, League City, Texas
(all grain)

Ingredients for 5 gallons

9	pounds pale malt
2	pounds crystal malt
1	ounce Perle hops (60 minutes)
1/2	ounce Hallertauer hops (30 minutes)
1/2	ounce Hallertauer hops (five minutes)
	Worthington White Shield yeast

Original specific gravity: 1.050
Final specific gravity: not given
Boiling time: 60 minutes
Primary fermentation: two weeks at 70 degrees F (21 degrees C) in stainless steel
Age when judged (since bottling): not given

Brewer's specifics

Force-carbonate; bottles filled with counter-pressure filler.

Judges' comments

"Grainy, malty, clean aroma. Good color, good head. Malty flavor, dry aftertaste."

"Malty bouquet. Brilliant appearance; could be a little darker. Good balance in flavor. Clean! Good job!"

"Minimal aroma, but contains some off characteristics. Appearance is a wee bit pale; brilliant clarity; good head retention. Good malt and hops flavor; very good balance; very good conditioning, very good aftertaste; diacetyl evident. Overall a good flavor profile. This is a well-balanced beer."

No. 69 Brown Ale

American Brown
Second Place, Brown Ale, 1991
Kenneth Cummings, Asheville, North Carolina
(all grain)

Ingredients for 5 gallons

6 1/4	*pounds Klages two-row malt*
1 3/4	*pounds 60 °L crystal malt*
1 1/4	*pounds dextrin six-row malt*
1/4	*pound chocolate two-row malt*
2/3	*ounce Northern Brewer hops, 6.7 percent alpha acid (60 minutes)*
1/2	*ounce Cascade hops, 5.4 percent alpha acid (60 minutes)*
1/4	*ounce Northern Brewer hops, 6.7 percent alpha acid (10 minutes)*
1/4	*ounce Cascade hops, 5.4 percent alpha acid (10 minutes)*
1/6	*ounce Northern Brewer hops, 6.7 percent alpha acid (one minute)*
1/6	*ounce Cascade hops, 5.4 percent alpha acid (one minute)*
1/3	*ounce Cascade hops, 5.4 percent alpha acid (dry)*
1/2	*teaspoon gypsum*
1/4	*teaspoon salt*
	M.eV. No. 87 English ale yeast
1/4	*teaspoon corn sugar per bottle to prime*

Original specific gravity: 1.045
Final specific gravity: 1.011
Boiling time: 60 minutes
Primary fermentation: nine days at 62 degrees F (17 degrees C) in glass
Secondary fermentation: 18 days at 62 degrees F (17 degrees C) in glass
Age when judged (since bottling): three months

Brewer's specifics

Mash grains for 40 minutes at 112 degrees F (44.5 degrees C). Raise temperature to 132 degrees F (55.5 degrees C) for 30 minutes. Raise again to 154 degrees F (68 degrees C) for 90 minutes. Sparge with 5 gallons of 168-degree-F (75.5-degree-C) water. Steep finish hops for 10 minutes before cooling wort.

Judges' comments

"Light on malt. Soft but plentiful hops. Good balance. Tiny (but good) DMS aftertaste."
"Light tan head. Very clear, dark mahogany color, good head, fair retention. Nice hoppy dark brew with well-balanced malt. Good brew. Great hop treatment."
"Great balance with good hop character. Slightly dry finish. Very tasty, good mouthfeel. Very smooth and satisfying. Excellent effort. Solid representation of style."

NOTES

Cedar Mountain Brown Ale

American Brown
Second Place, Brown Ale, 1993
Jim Dilldine, Craig, Colorado
(grain/extract)

Ingredients for 5 gallons

6 2/3	*pounds Northwestern Gold malt extract syrup*
1	*pound William's Australian dark dry malt extract*
6	*ounces chocolate malt*
6	*ounces roasted barley*
6	*ounces 80 °L crystal malt*
1	*ounce English Fuggles hops, 3.8 percent alpha acid (60 minutes)*
1	*ounce Northern Bullion hops, 7.9 percent alpha acid (60 minutes)*
1/2	*ounce English Fuggles hops, 3.8 percent alpha acid (10 minutes)*
1/2	*ounce Washington Cascade hops, 4.6 percent alpha acid (10 minutes)*
1/2	*ounce Washington Cascade hops, 4.6 percent alpha acid (end of boil)*
1	*teaspoon Irish moss*
	Wyeast No.1007 liquid yeast culture
7/8	*cup corn sugar to prime*

Original specific gravity: 1.056
Final specific gravity: 1.012
Boiling time: 60 minutes
Primary fermentation: seven days at 65 degrees F (18 degrees C) in plastic
Secondary fermentation: seven days at 65 degrees F (18 degrees C) in glass
Age when judged (since bottling): 4 1/2 months

Brewer's specifics

Steep grains while raising temperature to boiling, then remove grains.

Judges' comments

"Very hoppy. Could use a little more malt for sweetness. Dry mouthfeel."
"Slightly phenolic, good hopping. Could use more maltiness to balance hops."
"Slightly overhopped for style."
"Good beer, but needs more malt. Good attempt."
"Very good. Would like more malt flavor for better balance."

CHAPTER 4

PALE ALE

One of the all-time classic beer styles, pale ale is a favorite among homebrewers. English pale ale was developed in the 1700s as an alternative to the porter style popular at the time. India pale ale, a stronger version of the classic pale ale, was designed with a higher hopping level and higher alcohol content to withstand the months-long voyage to India. American-style ale is similar to classic English pale ale in most respects, except that North American varieties of hops are used. The best pale ales have a superb hop character in the aroma and flavor, with lots of fruity flavors and a clean, dry, malty finish.

AHA National Homebrew Competition Style Guidelines
English Pale Ale
a) **Classic English Pale Ale** – Pale to deep amber/copper. Low to medium maltiness. High hop bitterness. Medium hop flavor and aroma. Use of English hops such as Goldings, Fuggles, etc. Fruity/estery. Low diacetyl OK. Medium body.
b) **India Pale Ale** – Pale to deep amber/copper. Medium body. Medium maltiness. High hop bitterness. Hop flavor and aroma medium to high. Fruity/estery. Alcoholic strength evident. Low diacetyl OK.

NOTES

OG (Balling/Plato)	Percent alc./vol.	IBUs	SRM
a) Classic English Pale Ale			
1.044-56 (11-14)	4.5-5.5%	20-40	4-11
b) India Pale Ale			
1.050-65 (12.5-16)	5-6.5%	40-65	8-14

American Pale Ale

a) American Pale Ale – Pale to deep amber/red/copper. Low to medium maltiness. High hop bitterness. Medium hop flavor and aroma. Use of American hops such as Cascade, Willamette, Centennial (CFJ-90), etc. Fruity/estery. Low diacetyl OK. Medium body.

b) American Wheat – Pale to amber. Light to medium body. Low to medium bitterness. Malt and hop flavor and aroma OK. Low to medium fruitiness and esters. Low diacetyl OK. Lager yeast OK.

OG (Balling/Plato)	Percent alc./vol.	IBUs	SRM
a) American Pale Ale			
1.044-56 (11-14)	4.5-5.5%	20-40	4-11
b) American Wheat			
1.030-50 (7.5-12.5)	4.3-5.5%	5-17	2-8

34 PALE ALE   *Victory Beer Recipes*

CASCADE DELIGHT

Classic Pale Ale
First Place, English-style Pale Ale, 1990
Tom Cooper, Houston, Texas
(all grain)

Ingredients for 5 gallons

10	pounds Klages two-row malt
1/2	pound Munton and Fison medium crystal malt
3/4	ounce Cluster hops (60 minutes)
1/2	ounce Cascade hops (60 minutes)
1/2	ounce Cascade hops (30 minutes)
1	ounce Cascade hops (steep 30 minutes after boil)
1 1/2	ounce Cascade hops (dry hop)
1	teaspoon Irish moss
1	teaspoon gypsum
1/2	teaspoon citric acid
	Wyeast No. 1056 Chico Ale liquid yeast
3/4	cup dextrose to prime

Original specific gravity: 1.053
Final specific gravity: 1.010
Primary fermentation: eight days at 60 to 65 degrees F (15.5 to 18.5 degrees C) in glass
Secondary fermentation: 24 days at 65 to 68 degrees F (18.5 to 20 degrees C) in glass
Age when judged (since bottling): 3 1/2 months

Brewer's specifics

Mash for 90 minutes at 152 degrees F (66.5 degrees C). Mash out for 10 minutes at 170 degrees F (76.5 degrees C). Sparge with 170-degree-F (76.5-degree-C) water and collect 7 gallons.

Judges' comments

"Wonderful aroma! Good hop bouquet, with malt highlights sneaking in and out. Good color. Nice and clear; good head. Great flavor! Malt and hops both come through! Clean and balanced. Body is just right — beautiful! Overall this is very true to style and drinks quite nicely. Can you say Sierra Nevada?"

"Nice hoppy, estery nose. Clear, good head and carbonation. Nice malt-hop balance. Good body. Hops dominate. Great overall ale."

"Aroma is all hops, but no malt. Very clean. Some buttery notes but OK for category. Very pretty color, very good clarity, decent head retention. Light malt and excellent hop flavor. The hops come through stronger than the malt. Conditioning is appropriately light. Hops dominate the aftertaste. Body is a bit thin. Overall, this beer is very pleasant, but could use some more malt in finish and to help balance the hops."

HALF AND HALF ALE

Classic Pale Ale
First Place, English-style Pale Ale, 1989
Charles Milan, Baton Rouge, Louisiana
(grain/extract)

Ingredients for 6 gallons

3 1/3	pounds Munton and Fison light malt extract
1	pound Munton and Fison light dry malt extract
4	pounds Munton and Fison pale malt
1/2	pound Munton and Fison crystal malt
1/2	pound Williams Munich malt
1 3/4	ounces Northern Brewer hops (60 minutes)
1	teaspoon Irish moss (10 minutes)
1/2	ounce Saaz hops (10 minutes)
1/2	ounce Saaz hops (steep 30 minutes after boil)
2	teaspoons gypsum
	William's English Brewery yeast
1 1/4	cups amber diastatic malt extract to prime

Original specific gravity: 1.052
Final specific gravity: 1.017
Boiling time: 60 minutes
Primary fermentation: two weeks at 70 degrees F (21 degrees C) in plastic
Secondary fermentation: 12 days at 70 degrees F (21 degrees C) in glass
Age when judged (since bottling): three months

Brewer's specifics

Infusion mash: 150 to 160 degrees F (65.5 to 71 degrees C) for 1 1/2 hours. Sparge with 3 1/2 gallons 175-degree-F (79.5-degree-C) water.

Judges' comments

"Wonderful aroma. Appearance is good. Flavor is well-balanced. Overall an excellent brew; congratulations!"
"Estery aroma. Appearance is appropriate. Flavor is good overall, nicely balanced. Overall, very drinkable beer."

DIVING DUCK ALE

India Pale Ale
First Place, English-style Pale Ale, 1989
James T. Reese, Amarillo, Texas
(extract)

Ingredients for 5 gallons

3 1/3	pounds John Bull hopped malt extract
3	pounds Cooper's Bitter malt extract
2	pounds Brewmaster light dry malt extract
1	ounce Willamette hops (60 minutes)
1/2	ounce Kent Goldings hops (finish)
1	ounce Kent Goldings hops (dry)
4	ounces maltodextrin
1/2	teaspoon Irish moss
	Wyeast No. 1056 Chico Ale liquid yeast
3/4	cup corn sugar to prime

Original specific gravity: not given
Final specific gravity: not given
Boiling time: 60 minutes
Primary fermentation: four weeks at 65 degrees F (18.3 degrees C) in glass
Age when judged (since bottling): 2 1/2 months

Judges' comments

"Robust aroma. Clear. Robust flavor; good balance. Overall this is good beer!"
"Aroma is appropriate. Nice appearance. Very good flavor balance. Overall very drinkable; good overall."

HOSPITAL PALOR

India Pale Ale
First Place, English-style Pale Ale, 1991
Quentin Smith, Rohnert Park, California
(all grain)

Ingredients for 5 gallons

14	pounds Klages malt
4	ounces 40 °L crystal malt
4	ounces 90 °L crystal malt
2	teaspoons gypsum (in sparge)
1/2	teaspoon calcium carbonate (in sparge)
1/4	teaspoon non-iodized salt (in sparge)
1/2	ounce Nugget hops, 11.1 percent alpha acid (60 minutes)
1	ounce Perle hops, 6.3 percent alpha acid (30 minutes)
1	ounce Cascade hops, 4.9 percent alpha acid (30 minutes)
1	ounce Perle hops, 6.3 percent alpha acid (finish)
1	ounce Cascade hops, 4.9 percent alpha acid (finish)
	Wyeast No. 1056 liquid ale yeast
3/4	cup corn sugar to prime

Original specific gravity: 1.062
Final specific gravity: 1.010
Boiling time: 60 minutes
Age when judged (since bottling): three months

Brewer's specifics

Mash grains for 90 minutes at 150 degrees F (65.5 degrees C).
Mash-out at 170 degrees F (76.5 degrees C), sparge with 170-degree-F (76.5-degree-C) water.

Judges' comments

"Alcoholic, estery, and fruity aroma. Slight diacetyl, good balance, nice finish. Good body, needs to be dry hopped."
"Nice malt, slightly alcoholic aroma. Good color and clarity. Nice hop-malt balance. Good body. Nice beer! Alcoholic and warming in the finish."

THIRD FLOOR MILD ALE

American Pale Ale
Second Place, American-style Ale, 1992
Michael Chronister, Norristown, Pennsylvania
(all grain)

Ingredients for 5 gallons

5	pounds two-row mild ale malt
1	pound two-row pale ale malt
2	pounds two-row Munich malt
1	ounce Perle hops, 7.7 percent alpha acid (30 minutes)
2	ounces Cascade hops, 5.2 percent alpha acid (20 minutes)
	Leigh-William's beer and stout dried yeast
1	teaspoon gypsum
3/4	cup corn sugar to prime

Original specific gravity: 1.048
Final specific gravity: 1.014
Boiling time: 60 minutes
Primary fermentation: seven days at 62 to 64 degrees F (17 to 18 degrees C) in glass
Secondary fermentation: 10 days at 50 degrees F (10 degrees C) in glass
Age when judged (since bottling): six months

Brewer's specifics

Mash grains for 90 minutes at 152 degrees F (67 degrees C).
Sparge with 3 1/2 gallons 165-degree-F (74-degree-C) water.

Judges' comments

"A great beer. Needs to be bigger. Flavor is slightly laid back."
"Slightly metallic tinge to hop character — water? Otherwise pretty well balanced, nice beer. Could use a little more flavor hops."
"Good balance. Slight astringent aftertaste. Not a big problem, but watch your sparging if you mash."
"Slightly oxidized, body is good for style."

WHAMA JAMA

American Pale Ale
Third Place, American-style Ale, 1991
Rick and Barrie Mayer, Lake Zurich, Illinois
(all grain)

Ingredients for 5 gallons

7 3/4	pounds Klages malt
3/4	pound crystal malt
1/2	pound dextrin malt
2	ounces Cascade hops, 4.9 percent alpha acid (60 minutes)
2	ounces Kent Goldings hops, 4.7 percent alpha acid (10 minutes)
	Wyeast American ale liquid yeast
1	teaspoon gypsum
2/3	cup dextrose to prime

Original specific gravity: 1.043
Final specific gravity: 1.012
Boiling time: 60 minutes
Primary fermentation: 11 days at 65 degrees F (18.5 degrees C) in glass
Age when judged (since bottling): two months

Brewers' specifics

Mash grains at 122 degrees F (50 degrees C) for 50 minutes. Raise temperature to 158 degrees F (70 degrees C) and hold for 35 minutes. Sparge with 4 1/2 gallons of 165-degree-F (74-degree-C) water.

Judges' comments

"Fruity, flowery aroma with some diacetyl. Fair balance, condition good for style, astringent mouthfeel. Body seems thin. Cut back on bittering hops."

"Buttery fruit aroma. Nice hop bitterness — nice finish in the aftertaste. Nice body. A very drinkable beer but almost seems more a classic pale ale than an American pale ale."

American Wheat
First Place, American-style Ale, 1993
Jack H. Denny, Lenexa, Kansas
(all grain)

Ingredients for 5 gallons

4	pounds barley malt
4 1/2	pounds wheat malt
1/2	pound CaraPils malt
1/2	ounce Hallertauer hops, 4.8 percent alpha acid (60 minutes)
1/2	ounce Hallertauer hops, 4.8 percent alpha acid (40 minutes)
1/4	ounce Hallertauer hops, 4.1 percent alpha acid (20 minutes)
1/4	ounce Hallertauer hops, 4.1 percent alpha acid (two minutes)
	EDME ale yeast
2/3	cup corn sugar to prime

Original specific gravity: 1.046
Final specific gravity: 1.020
Boiling time: 120 minutes
Primary fermentation: 13 days at 66 to 68 degrees F (19 to 20 degrees C)
Age when judged (since bottling): 19 months

Brewer's specifics

Mash grains at 122 degrees F (50 degrees C) for 32 minutes. Raise to 145 degrees F (63 degrees C) for 20 minutes. Raise to 158 degrees F (70 degrees C) until conversion. Sparge with 4 1/2 gallons of 165-degree-F (74-degree-C) water.

Judges' comments

"Well-balanced, slight citric flavor but not tart. Fairly sweet but not cloying. Very good beer, no flaws."

"Smooth taste, but I'm looking for the wheat notes. Some diacetyl evident, OK for style. Hops are still neutral, which is OK for style. A fine beer."

"This is a well-made American wheat. The lemony character comes through nicely. A bit of hop character in the nose would add to this."

"Malty flavor comes right out. Good conditioning. I would try a few more IBUs in the kettle. Very nice beer."

"Hint of DMS in aroma. Lots of wheat flavor, low hop bitterness. Slight fruitiness is nice."

CHAPTER 5

ENGLISH BITTER AND SCOTTISH ALE

English bitter is a mainstay beer in English pubs. Unlike the name suggests, it is not inordinately bitter in character. Traditionally, bitters were cask conditioned beers, of fairly low alcohol to facilitate session consumption. Overall, bitters should be well-balanced between hop, malt, and fruity yeast flavors. The principal difference between the three common English bitters is increasingly assertive malt and hop flavors, and higher alcohol levels in the special and extra special bitters. Because these ales were, and still are, often served from casks with hand-pumped beer engines, a low carbonation level will lend authenticity to your homebrewed bitters.

Scottish ales are similar to English bitter, except that they have lower levels of yeast flavors, are maltier in character, and are a little more roasty in flavor.

AHA National Homebrew Competition Style Guidelines
English Bitter
Gold to copper. Low carbonation. Medium bitterness. May or may not have hop flavor or aroma. Low to medium maltiness. Light to medium body. Low to medium diacetyl OK. Fruitiness/esters OK.
a) **English Ordinary** – Mildest.
b) **English Special** – Moderate strength. Maltiness more evident along with increased hop character.
c) **English Extra Special** – Strong bitter. Maltiness evident. Hop bitterness balanced with malt sweetness.

OG (Balling/Plato)	Percent alc./vol.	IBUs	SRM
a) English Ordinary			
1.035-38 (8.5-9.5)	3-3.5%	20-25	8-12
b) English Special			
1.038-42 (9.5-10.5)	3.5-4.5%	25-30	12-14
c) English Extra Special			
1.042-55 (10.5-13.5)	4.5-6%	30-35	12-14

Scottish Ale

a) Scottish Light – Gold to amber. Low carbonation. Low bitterness. May or may not have hop flavor and aroma. Medium maltiness. Medium body. Low to medium diacetyl OK. Fruitiness/esters OK. Faint smoky character OK.

b) Scottish Heavy – Gold to amber to dark brown. Low carbonation. Low bitterness. May or may not have hop flavor and aroma. Medium to high maltiness. Medium body. Low to medium diacetyl OK. Fruitiness/esters OK. Faint smoky character OK.

c) Scottish Export – Gold to amber to dark brown. Low carbonation. Low to medium bitterness. May or may not have hop flavor and aroma. High maltiness. Medium to high body. Low to medium diacetyl OK. Fruitiness/esters OK. Faint smoky character OK.

OG (Balling/Plato)	Percent alc/vol.	IBUs	SRM
a) Scottish Light			
1.030-35 (7.5-9)	3-4%	9-15	8-17
b) Scottish Heavy			
1.035-40 (9-10)	3.5-4%	12-17	10-19
c) Scottish Export			
1.040-50 (10-12.5)	4-4.5%	15-20	10-19

QUICK AND DIRTY

British Bitter
First Place, Pale Ale*, 1990
Ron Page, Middletown, Connecticut
(all grain)

Ingredients for 23 gallons

35	pounds Munton and Fison two-row malt
5	pounds Briess two-row malt
3	pounds crystal malt
2	pounds CaraPils malt
4 1/2	ounces Kent Goldings hops (60 minutes)
4	ounces Cascade hops (60 minutes)
	Lager yeast from New England Brewing Company

Original specific gravity: 1.046
Final specific gravity: not given
Primary fermentation: eight days at 58 degrees F (14.5 degrees C) in glass
Secondary fermentation: three days at 40 degrees F (4.5 degrees C) in glass
Age when judged (since bottling): three months

Brewer's specifics

Mash for 90 minutes at 150 degrees F (65.5 degrees C). Forced CO_2 (15 pounds) to carbonate.

Judges' comments

"Aroma is an excellent combination of malt and hops. No fault in appearance. Flavor has a good balance of hops-to-malt sweetness. Could be better with less malt sweetness. Body is too full. Overall this beer is near perfect. May be improved by using a more attenuating yeast, and then fewer hops to balance."

"Unusual aroma. I've come across this before when hops are left in contact with the beer too long. Flavor has a good balance; pleasant aftertaste, fruity. Body good for style. Apart from what's mentioned above, I can't find fault in this beer. Fruity flavor acceptable for style."

"Nice aroma. Overall excellent appearance. Nice body. Nice beer. Aroma and palate are fine!"

*In 1989 and 1990, the Pale Ale category had three subcategoris: Old Pale Ale/Classic Pale Ale, Pale Ale/India Pale Ale, and Pale Ale/British Bitter. First-, second-, and third-place awards were given in each subcategory.

CASCADE BITTER

British Bitter
First Place, Pale Ale*, 1989
Norman Hardy, Seattle, Washington
(all grain)

Ingredients for 5 gallons

8	pounds Klages malt
8	ounces crystal malt
2	ounces Cascade hop pellets (45 minutes)
1	ounce Rogers Goldings hops (simmered 15 minutes)
8	ounces brown sugar
2	teaspoons gypsum
	Wyeast No. 1028 British Ale liquid yeast
2/3	cup corn sugar to prime

Original specific gravity: 1.046
Final specific gravity: 1.013
Boiling time: 75 minutes
Primary fermentation: three weeks at 65 degrees F (18.5 degrees C) in glass
Secondary fermentation: 12 days at 65 degrees F (18.5 degrees C) in glass
Age when judged (since bottling): two months

Brewer's specifics

Step-infusion mash at 132 to 136 degrees F (55.5 to 58 degrees C) for 60 minutes (2 1/8 gallons); 150 to 152 degrees F (65.5 to 67 degrees C) for 15 minutes (3 gallons); 152 to 158 degrees F (67 to 70 with degrees C) for 55 minutes; 168 degrees F (75.5 degrees C) for five minutes. Sparge with 168-degree-F (75.5-degree-C) water.

Judges' comments

"Very nice hop aroma followed by malt. Good color. Excellent head retention — maintained for 15 minutes. Very clear, well-balanced beer. An excellent beer."

"Hop nose comes through clean with good malt aroma. If anything, maybe a little more finishing hops. Color and clarity excellent. Flavor has great balance between malt and hops, no graininess evident. Very drinkable; no off-flavors. Well crafted. Keep up the good brewing techniques."

"Aroma is fruity. Malt and hops are balanced nicely. Very clear beer. Excellent flavor balance, clean. Excellent overall product. Keep up the good work."

*In 1989 and 1990, the Pale Ale category had three subcategoris: Old Pale Ale/Classic Pale Ale, Pale Ale/India Pale Ale, and Pale Ale/British Bitter. First-, second-, and third-place awards were given in each subcategory.

CAROLINE'S MILD

English Ordinary
First Place, English Bitter, 1992
John Arends, Calistoga, California
(all grain)

Ingredients for 10 gallons

15 1/2	pounds Klages malt
1	pound 40 °L crystal malt
3/4	pound 90 °L crystal malt
1/2	pound wheat malt
1/2	pound CaraPils malt
1 1/3	ounces Kent Goldings hops, 4.9 percent alpha acid (60 minutes)
1 1/2	ounces Kent Goldings hops, 4.9 percent alpha acid (30 minutes)
1 1/10	ounces Kent Goldings hops, 4.9 percent alpha acid (two minutes)
1/2	teaspoon gypsum
1/2	teaspoon chalk
1/4	teaspoon salt
	Wyeast No. 1028 liquid yeast
1 1/2	cups corn sugar to prime

Original specific gravity: 1.038
Final specific gravity: 1.011
Boiling time: 60 minutes
Primary fermentation: nine days at 68 degrees F (20 degrees C) in glass
Secondary fermentation: 13 days at 68 degrees F (20 degrees C) in glass
Age when judged (since bottling): three months

Brewer's specifics

Mash grains for 75 minutes at 156 degrees F (69 degrees C).
Sparge with 175-degree-F (79-degree-C) water.

Judges' comments

"Touch of hops and malt — very nice. Subtle. Very good for an ordinary bitter. I wish I'd brewed this — wonderful job! Thanks!"
"Almost the perfect beer. Could perhaps use a bit more hop bitterness."
"This is no ordinary beer. Excellent. Would be hard to improve."
"Malty, some caramel, good hop balance. Clean finish, nice conditioning. A little bold for an ordinary bitter. Might fit special bitter style better."

NOTES

BRIDGE HOUSE BITTER

English Special
First Place, English Bitter, 1991
Andy Leith, St. Louis, Missouri
(all grain)

Ingredients for 5 gallons
9	pounds pale ale malt
8	ounces 60 °L crystal malt
1 3/4	ounce Willamette hops (90 minutes)
1/2	ounce Fuggles hops (90 minutes)
1	ounce Goldings hops (finish)
	Wyeast Irish ale liquid yeast

Original specific gravity: 1.042
Final specific gravity: 1.010
Boiling time: 90 minutes
Primary fermentation: four days
Secondary fermentation: 10 days
Age when judged (since bottling): not given

Brewer's specifics
Mash grains with 12 quarts water for 30 minutes at 125 degrees F (51.5 degrees C). Raise temperature to 154 degrees F (68 degrees F) and hold for 90 minutes. The sparge was conducted very quickly, hence the large amount of grain used.

Judges' comments
"Gentle and kind hop and malt aroma. A nice balance has been struck here, a good rosy drinking beer — what a bitter should be, no off-flavors detected."
"Some DMS initially, faded. Floral hop character, some malt evident. Very nice flavor, excellent British-style carbonation. Well-balanced, pleasant aftertaste."
"Outstandingly English! The only thing missing is the hand-pump and the public bar footrail to stand on!"

CHAPTER 6

PORTER

One of the oldest beer styles in the world, porter is a deep red, somewhat sweet beer, with a rich caramelly and chocolatey character. Its origins, and an uncontroversial definition of the style, are difficult to uncover. Legend has it that drinkers in the 1700s mixed different beers together to achieve a pleasing flavor. A brewer named Harwood developed a drink he called "entire," which "premixed" the popular flavor. Ironically, we do not know exactly what the 18th century version of porter tasted like, because brewing records of the time are not explicit. Regardless of porter's ambiguous roots, it has become a welcome and popular addition to the homebrewing repertoire.

AHA National Homebrew Competition Style Guidelines
a) **Robust Porter** – Black. No roast barley character. Sharp bitterness of black malt without high burnt/charcoallike flavor. Medium to full bodied. Malty sweet. Hop bitterness medium to high. Hop flavor and aroma: none to medium. Fruitiness/esters OK. Low diacetyl OK.
b) **Brown Porter** – Medium to dark brown. No roast barley or strong burnt malt character. Light to medium body. Low to medium malt sweetness. Medium hop bitterness. Hop flavor and aroma: none to medium. Fruitiness/esters OK. Low diacetyl OK.

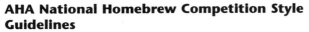

OG (Balling/Plato)	Percent alc./vol.	IBUs	SRM
a) Robust Porter			
1.044-60 (11-15)	5-6.5%	25-40	30+
b) Brown Porter			
1.040-50 (10-12.5)	4.5-6%	20-30	20-35

COAL PORTER

Brown Porter
First Place, Porter, 1992
Dennis Kinvig, Toronto, Ontario
(grain/extract)

Ingredients for 5 gallons

3 1/3	pounds Brewmaker Mild hopped malt extract
3 1/3	pounds Munton and Fison amber malt extract
1 2/3	pounds caramel malt
5	ounces chocolate malt
1/2	ounce Northern Brewer hops, 8 percent alpha acid (35 minutes)
1/4	ounce Northern Brewer hops, 8 percent alpha acid (two minutes)
1/4	ounce Cascade hops (dry)
1/2	ounce Hallertauer hops (dry)
6	ounces barley syrup
	Wyeast No. 1084 liquid yeast
1/2	teaspoon non-iodized salt
3 3/4	ounces dextrose to prime

Primary fermentation: 12 days at 65 degrees F (18 degrees C) in plastic
Age when judged (since bottling): four months

Brewer's specifics

Steep grains until boiling, then remove.

Judges' comments

"Slight burnt malt aroma. Smooth flavor, slight burnt malt flavor. Clean. Good example of brown porter."
"A touch smoky-phenolic, otherwise sweet and inviting. Very clean, almost lagerlike. Good creamy head."
"Lovely rich brown color. A bit husky, but I get no diacetyl. Good rich taste for style but a bit too bitter. A proud entry."
"Really well-balanced ale. Body just a little over medium."

PRANCING PONY PORTER

Porter
Second Place, Porter, 1989
Craig Olzenak, Grinnell, Iowa
(grain/extract)

Ingredients for 5 gallons

6	pounds Munton and Fison dark dry malt extract
1 1/2	pounds crystal malt
1/2	pound black patent malt
1 1/2	ounces Galena hops (45 minutes)
1/2	ounce Cascade hop pellets (dry)
1/2	ounce Northern Brewer hop pellets (dry)
1	teaspoon gypsum
1	teaspoon Irish moss
4	ounces maltodextrin
2	packets Red Star lager yeast
1/2	cup dextrose to prime
1/4	cup dark brown sugar to prime

Original specific gravity: 1.052
Final specific gravity: not given
Boiling time: 45 minutes
Primary fermentation: three weeks at 54 to 64 degrees F (12 to 18 degrees C) in plastic
Secondary fermentation: 12 days at 54 to 64 degrees F (12 to 18 degrees C) in glass
Age when judged (since bottling): two months

Brewer's specifics

Add finishing (dry) hops with yeast.

Judges' comments

"Nice aroma. Good appearance. Good flavor; needs more caramel malt to balance the bittering. Overall, a good beer. Could use some more malt and a little more body."

"Hoppy, nice aroma (alcoholic?). Mild, mellow, well-balanced flavor. A mild porter. A bit bitter, but I like that."

"Fruity, roasted, clean and pleasant aroma. Good all-around appearance. Flavor lacks malt sweetness to balance roast flavor. Overall a good, drinkable beer. Could use more malt body."

Porter
First Place, Porter, 1990
Paddy Giffen, Cotati, California
(all grain)

Ingredients for 5 gallons

5	pounds British pale malt
4	pounds Klages malt
1 1/2	pounds Vienna malt
1	pound 90 °L crystal malt
1	pound chocolate malt
1/2	pound CaraPils malt
1/4	pound black patent malt
1/4	ounce Northern Brewer hops (60 minutes)
1/4	ounce Perle hops (60 minutes)
3/4	ounce Chinook hops (30 minutes)
1	ounce Cascade hops (30 minutes)
1	ounce Cascade hops (dry hop in primary)
	Brewer's Choice No. 1084 Irish stout liquid yeast
2/3	cup corn sugar for priming

Original specific gravity: 1.057
Final specific gravity: 1.021
Primary fermentation: seven days at 65 degrees F (18.5 degrees C) in glass
Secondary fermentation: six weeks at 65 degrees F (18.5 degrees C) in glass
Age when judged (since bottling): 2 1/2 months

Brewer's specifics

One step infusion mash. Mash British pale, Klages, Vienna, CaraPils, and 3/4 pound crystal malts at 158 degrees F (70 degrees C) for 60 minutes. Crack and steep chocolate, black patent, and 1/4 pound crystal malts in 1 gallon of cold water, bring to a boil, then sparge with 1 pint 170-degree-F (76.5-degree-C) water.

Judges' comments

"A little buttery-caramel in nose. Pleasant, balanced. Very dark for style. Nice head. Lots of CO_2 — good head retention. Nice roasted character. Good chocolate taste. Hops balanced with sweetness. Good full body. A fine example of the style. Very full and well-balanced. Buttery taste evident but doesn't detract."

"Slightly phenolic, but good malt aroma with appropriate hoppiness. Beautiful head retention. Creamy crown. Nice color. Very slightly sour aftertaste. Overall a fine beer. Rich body. Almost too dark, but I like that. A great porter. Good beer!"

"Roast, fruity, hoppy in a nice balance; some diacetyl. Good head. Soft, well-balanced, clean. A bit lacking in depth of roasted character. Some sweetness. Full-bodied. A very satisfying beer, but a bit on the brown-aleish side. A bit more roast character would help."

PETER'S PORTER

Robust Porter
Second Place, Porter, 1992
Jack Spence, Alexandria, Virginia
(all grain)

Ingredients for 5 gallons

8	pounds pale ale malt
1	pound 120 °L crystal malt
1	pound CaraPils malt
1/2	pound chocolate malt
1/2	pound black malt
1	ounce Chinook hops, 11.3 percent alpha acid (60 minutes)
1	ounce Cascade hops, 5.9 percent alpha acid (30 minutes)
1 1/3	ounce Cascade hops, 11.3 percent alpha acid (30 minutes)
	Brewer's Choice Altbier yeast culture
3/4	cup dextrose to prime

Original specific gravity: 1.057
Final specific gravity: 1.008
Boiling time: 60 minutes
Primary fermentation: four days at 68 degrees F (20 degrees C) in glass
Secondary fermentation: 14 days at 68 degrees F (20 degrees C) in glass
Age when judged (since bottling): five months

Brewer's specifics

Mash grains at 158 degrees F (70 degrees C) for 90 minutes.

Judges' comments

"Clean, hoppy, malty, lingering sweet taste."
"Sour, phenolic taste covers toast of malt. Well-conditioned, good chocolatey aftertaste. A proud entry. Delightful overall."
"Good use of dark grains, the touch of roasted barley is appropriate. Good balance, well-crafted. Back off the roasted barley for lighter color."
"Smooth, slight bitterness from black patent malt. Clean medium hop bitterness."

CREAM CITY PORTER

Brown Porter
First Place, Porter, 1991
Robert Burko, Milwaukee, Wisconsin
(all grain)

Ingredients for 5 gallons

9	pounds British pale ale malt
3	pounds British brown malt
3/4	pound crystal malt
1/2	pound chocolate malt
1/2	pound wheat malt
3/4	ounce Perle hops, 7.9 percent alpha acid (60 minutes)
1/2	ounce Willamette hops, 4.7 percent alpha acid (60 minutes)
1	ounce Willamette hops, 4.7 percent alpha acid (15 minutes)
1/2	ounce Perle hops, 7.9 percent alpha acid (one minute)
1	tablespoon Irish moss (15 minutes)
	Wyeast No. 1056 liquid ale yeast
1/4	cup dextrose to prime

Original specific gravity: 1.056
Final specific gravity: 1.018
Boiling time: 60 minutes
Primary fermentation: 22 days at 58 degrees F (14.5 degrees C) in glass
Age when judged (since bottling): four months

Brewer's specifics

Mash with 4 1/2 gallons of water at 168 degrees F (75.5 degrees C). Mash grains in a single-step infusion at 154 degrees F (68 degrees C) for two hours at pH 5.4. Sparge with 5 1/2 gallons of water.

Judges' comments

"Hoppy brown porter, but nice. Increase residual malt slightly to get closer to brown porter. Bitterness seems slightly high for a brown porter. Hops and malt meld nicely."

"Flavor is good, nice finish, perhaps a touch more chocolate malt to round out the flavor. A well-made beer."

"Malt is just a bit burnt in the nose. Hops are just great. Nothing off. Malt taste is great, but a little too strong, throwing off the balance. Body rich and full — a good-feeling beer."

TGI PORTER

Porter
Second Place, Porter, 1990
Cory Bailey, Sandy, Utah
(all grain)

Ingredients for 5 gallons

8	*pounds two-row malt*
1	*pound Munich malt*
1/2	*pound crystal malt*
1/2	*pound black patent malt*
1/2	*pound chocolate malt*
1	*ounce Bullion hops (60 minutes)*
1/2	*ounce Cascade hops (60 minutes)*
1/2	*ounce Cascade hops (two minutes)*
1	*teaspoon gypsum*
1/4	*teaspoon Irish moss*
	Cultured Sierra Nevada yeast in a one-pint starter
3/4	*cup dextrose to prime*

Original specific gravity: 1.057
Final specific gravity: not given
Boiling time: 60 minutes
Primary fermentation: two days at 70 degrees F (21 degrees C) in glass
Secondary fermentation: six days at 66 degrees F (19 degrees C) in glass
Age when judged (since bottling): three months

Brewer's specifics

Add 2 1/2 gallons of water at 130 degrees F (54.5 degrees C) to grain. Hold at 122 degrees F (50 degrees C) for 30 minutes, then add 5 quarts of 208-degree-F (98-degree-C) water to raise the temperature to 144 degrees F (62 degrees C). Raise temperature to 154 degrees F (68 degrees C) and hold for 10 minutes. Raise temperature to 158 degrees F (70 degrees C) and hold until conversion. Raise temperature to 170 degrees F (76.5 degrees C) and lauter. Sparge with 4 1/2 gallons of 170-degree-F (76.5-degree-C) water.

Judges' comments

"Fruity, herbal aroma, later a bit sherrylike. Good balance, smooth, slightly sticky texture. Well balanced, with alcohol a bit high for the style."
"Beautiful beer, hard to fault. Body is, if anything, light, but not too light. A very fine porter — I'd like to have more."
"Good roast in aroma, little hops, clean. Good balance, slightly old (some oxidation in aftertaste). Overall a very good porter, on the alcoholic side, which masks other flavor components."

CHAPTER 7

ENGLISH AND SCOTTISH STRONG ALE

Another of the world's older beer styles, English and Scottish strong ales are high in alcohol, strong in malt sweetness, and fairly heavy in body. Lots of fruity and estery yeast flavors should be present, and hop character should be just enough to keep the malt sweetness from being too cloying. Scotch ale in particular should have an almost overwhelming malt character, and sometimes can be syrupy in body. A very slight roastiness is acceptable in these beers.

AHA National Homebrew Competition Style Guidelines
a) English Old Ale/Strong Ale – Light amber to deep amber/copper. Medium to full body. Malty. Hop bitterness apparent but not aggressive, flavor and aroma can be assertive. Fruitiness/esters high. Alcoholic strength recognizable. Low diacetyl OK.
b) Strong "Scotch" Ale – Similar to English Old Ale/Strong Ale. Stronger, malty character. Deep copper to very black. Hop bitterness low. Diacetyl medium to high.

OG (Balling/Plato)	Percent alc./vol.	
IBUs	**SR**	
a) English Old Ale /Strong Ale		
1.060-75 (15-19)	6.5-8.5%	30
b) Strong "Scotch" Ale		
1.072-85 (18-21)	6.2-8%	25

SCOTCH ALE

Strong "Scotch" Ale
First Place, English and Scottish Strong Ale, 1990
Jerry Bockmore, Dayton, Oregon
(all grain)

Ingredients for 5 gallons

3 1/2	pounds mild ale malt
3	pounds Klages malt
3	pounds pale ale malt
2	pounds British crystal malt
2	ounces chocolate malt
2	ounces black patent malt
1	ounce Chinook hops (60 minutes)
1/2	ounce Goldings hops (60 minutes)
1	ounce Goldings hops (10 minutes)
1	pound dark brown sugar
1	teaspoon gypsum
1	teaspoon Burton salts
1	quart Wyeast No. 1028 British Ale liquid yeast starter
3/4	cup dextrose to prime

Original specific gravity: 1.063
Final specific gravity: 1.020
Primary fermentation: three weeks at 65 degrees F (18.5 degrees C) in glass
Age when judged (since bottling): 3 1/2 months

Brewer's specifics

Mash for 60 minutes at 154 degrees F (68 degrees C).

Judges' comments

"Very faint malt aroma. Clear appearance, nice head, color OK. Flavor is balanced and fair, good quality malt, a bit astringent. Full body. Overall a nice brew."

"Nice fruity nose. Big, long-lasting head. Slight haze, but OK. Sweetness and hops come to a good balance in flavor, but a dryer finish would be more appealing. Nice soft body, but a little light for the category. Very nice all around. Might be a bit bigger and a little dryer."

"Nice malty aroma. Color, clarity and head retention all very good. Good balance and aftertaste. Good body. Overall a very drinkable beer. A very good beer. Good work."

BEAM ME UP, SCOTTY

Strong "Scotch" Ale
Second Place, English and Scottish Strong Ale, 1989
Robert Burko, Milwaukee, Wisconsin
(grain/extract)

Ingredients for 5 gallons

5	pounds Diamalt light malt extract
5	pounds Diamalt amber malt extract
1	pound caramel malt
2	ounces chocolate malt
2	ounces Oregon Fuggles hop pellets (60 minutes)
1/2	ounce Styrian Golding hop pellets (30 minutes)
1/4	ounce Willamette hops (10 minutes)
2	teaspoons gypsum
1	tablespoon Irish moss
	Wyeast Irish ale yeast
3/4	cup corn sugar to prime

Original specific gravity: 1.070
Final specific gravity: not given
Boiling time: 75 minutes
Primary fermentation: 1 1/2 weeks at 68 degrees F (20 degrees C) in glass
Age when judged (since bottling): 4 1/2 months

Brewer's specifics

Add grains to 6 gallons cold water. Bring to boil and remove grains just before boiling.

Judges' comments

"Good malty aroma; good fruitiness for style. A bit too dark, but clear. Good flavor; malty; very well balanced. Very drinkable; very close to style."

"Nice malty and fruity aroma. Cleanly brewed. Nice rocky head, with good retention. Nice initial sweetness; finish is a little on the watery side. Overall a nice beer; true to style. Well done."

"Complex malt, fruity esters in aroma with nice interplay of hops in good proportion for style. Good head retention; a bit dark for category. Flavor is well balanced, but could use a bit more malt identity; hops take over finish. Overall, good effort with a complex nose and nice conditioning. Beef up the malt character."

FIFTY-SIX POUND ALE

Strong "Scotch" Ale
Second Place, English and Scottish Strong Ale, 1990
Kelly Robinson, Ceres, California
(grain/extract)

Ingredients for 5 gallons

13	pounds pale ale malt
3	pounds Alexander's light malt extract
1/2	pound crystal malt
1/2	pound toasted pale malt
5	ounces Munich malt
4	ounces black patent malt
1	pound brown sugar
1 1/2	ounces Willamette hops (60 minutes)
1/4	ounce Fuggles hops (60 minutes)
1/2	ounce Willamette hops (30 minutes)
3/4	ounce Northern Brewer hops (30 minutes)
1/2	ounce Perle hops (dry)
1/2	ounce Mount Hood hops (dry)
	Wyeast No. 1098 liquid yeast in three-cup starter

Original specific gravity: 1.092
Final specific gravity: 1.025
Boiling time: 135 minutes
Primary fermentation: seven days at 65 degrees F (18.5 degrees C) in glass
Secondary fermentation: 3 1/2 weeks at 50 degrees F (10 degrees C) in glass
Age when judged (since bottling): five months

Brewer's specifics

Toast 1/2 pound of pale malt at 375 degrees F (190 degrees C) for 10 minutes. Mash grains 90 minutes at 149 degrees F (65 degrees C). Sparge with 4 gallons of 170-degree-F (76.5-degree-C) water.

Judges' comments

"Very buttery, almost too much for style. Nice color. Exceptionally sweet, almost cloying. Very high alcohol. This is really one to sip, but the candylike sweetness is off-putting."

"Malty nose. Nice color, clear, fine head retention. Chewy, sherrylike finish, but balanced well. A bit phenolic from high alcohol. Well-done, powerful beer, but is it too big?"

"Soft, malty sweet and strawberrylike estery aroma. Inviting hops in the background. Body blew my kilt up! A brew any true Celt or Scot would take the high road or the low road to sip. Fine effort!"

K.A.

English Old Ale/Strong Ale
Third Place, English and Scottish Strong Ale, 1991
Sandra Castro and Helen Murphy, Sacramento, California
(all grain)

Ingredients for 10 gallons

28	pounds two-row malt
1 1/2	pounds Munich malt
2	pounds crystal malt
1/2	pound chocolate malt
3/4	ounce Cascade hops (60 minutes)
3/4	ounce Fuggles hops (60 minutes)
3/4	ounce Cascade hops (30 minutes)
3/4	ounce Fuggles hops (30 minutes)
2	ounces Cascade hops (finish)
2	ounces Fuggles hops (finish)
	Rubicon yeast culture

Original specific gravity: 1.066
Final specific gravity: not given
Boiling time: 60 minutes
Primary fermentation: 11 days at 60 to 65 degrees F (15 to 18 degrees C) in glass
Age when judged (since bottling): not given

Brewers' specifics

Mash grains at 155 degrees F (68 degrees C) for 60 minutes.

Judges' comments

"Very dry finish to beer. Slight overcarbonation washes away taste. Needs more hop-malt balance."
"Nice malty beer. Somewhat tart or bitter. Good beer."
"Fine beer though too hoppy for style. Clean, no problems other than balance."

A Peek Under the Kilt Ale

Strong "Scotch" Ale
First Place, English and Scottish Strong Ale, 1992
Jim Campbell, San Jose, California
(grain/extract)

Ingredients for 5 gallons

3 1/3	pounds amber malt extract syrup
6	pounds California light malt extract syrup
1	pound Australian light dry malt extract
2	pounds crystal malt
1/2	pound Munich malt
1/2	pound flaked barley
1/2	pound wheat malt
1/2	cup roasted barley
3/4	ounce Chinook hops (75 minutes)
1	ounce Hallertauer hops (75 minutes)
1	ounce Cascade hops (30 minutes)
1	ounce Kent Goldings hops (10 minutes)
1	ounce Cascade hops (five minutes)
1/2	teaspoon gypsum
1/2	teaspoon salt
1/2	teaspoon Irish moss
1/2	teaspoon ascorbic acid
	Sierra Nevada Celebration Ale yeast culture
3/4	cup corn sugar to prime

Original specific gravity: 1.074
Final specific gravity: 1.018
Boiling time: 75 minutes
Primary fermentation: 38 days at 65 degrees F (18 degrees C) in glass
Age when judged (since bottling): 12 months

Brewer's specifics

Steep all grains.

Judges' comments

"Good, well-made beer, but aggressive hopping isn't appropriate for style. Nice smokiness."

"Enjoyable, smooth beer. Huge flavor. Perhaps too much hoppiness for style."

"Malty aroma follows through to palate. Slightly smoky finish lends interest and complexity. A well-made beer."

"Overall a very nice effort, but too much hoppiness for style."

CHAPTER 8

STOUT

Stout should be as opaque and black in color as you can manage. Originally just a stronger version of porter, "stout porter" eventually became a popular style in its own right. Dry stout, of which draft Guinness is the world-class example, should have an assertive, dry-roasted finish, with minimal hop aroma, albeit a level of hop bitterness that balances the malt. Foreign-style stout is similar to dry stout, with a higher alcohol content. Sweet stout, sometimes called cream stout and milk stout, is one of the most full-bodied beers you can make. Lots of residual sugar and unfermentable ingredients, coupled with the occasional use of lactose (milk sugar), produces a heavy sweet brew that's almost a meal in itself. Imperial stout, as the story goes, was brewed for the Russian imperial court — its high alcohol content enabling the brew to withstand export. Imperial stouts should be lighter in color than other stout styles, and, of course, have a level of alcohol comparable to barley wines.

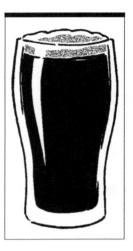

AHA National Homebrew Competition Style Guidelines
a) **Classic Dry Stout** – Black opaque. Light to medium body. Medium to high hop bitterness. Roasted barley (coffeelike) character required. Sweet maltiness and caramel malt evident. No hop flavor or aroma. Slight acidity/sourness OK. Low to medium alcohol. Low to medium diacetyl.
b) **Foreign Style** – Stronger version of classic dry stout.
c) **Sweet Stout** – Overall sweet character. Black

opaque. Medium to full body. Hop bitterness low. Roasted barley (coffeelike) character mild. No hop flavor or aroma. Sweet malty and caramel flavors evident. Low to medium alcohol. Low diacetyl OK.

d) Imperial Stout – Dark copper to black. Hop bitterness, flavor and aroma medium to high. Alcohol strength evident. Rich maltiness. Fruitiness/esters OK. Full bodied. Low diacetyl OK.

OG (Balling/Plato)	Percent alc./vol.	IBUs	SRM
a) Classic Dry Stout			
1.038-48 (9.5-12)	3.8-5%	30-40	40+
b) Foreign-style			
1.052-72 (13-18)	6-7.5%	30-60	40+
c) Sweet Stout			
1.045-56 (11-14)	3-6%	15-25	40+
d) Imperial Stout			
1.075-95 (19-23.5)	7-9%	50-80	20+

FOUNTAINHEAD BLACK MAGIC

Imperial Stout
First Place, Stout, 1989
Rande L. Reed, Milwaukee, Wisconsin
(grain/extract)

Ingredients for 2 1/2 gallons

3 1/3	pounds Munton and Fison Old Ale kit malt extract
2 1/2	pounds Munton and Fison light dry malt extract
6	ounces black patent malt
6	ounces roasted barley
6	ounces 40 °L caramel malt
1 1/2	ounces Nugget hops (60 minutes)
1/2	ounce Nugget hops (10 minutes)
1 1/2	teaspoons gypsum
1	packet Red Star Champagne yeast
2	ounces corn sugar to prime

Original specific gravity: 1.101
Final specific gravity: 1.036
Boiling time: 60 minutes
Primary fermentation: seven weeks at 70 degrees F (21 degrees C) in glass
Secondary fermentation: six weeks at 70 degrees F (21 degrees C) in glass
Age when judged (since bottling): four months

Brewer's specifics

Crush grains and add to 3 quarts cold water. Slowly raise temperature to gentle simmer and hold for 10 minutes. Sparge with 2 quarts hot water. Add to brewpot to make 3 gallons total liquid. Heat to boil and add malt extract.

Judges' comments

"Diacetyl and malty aroma OK for style; pleasant. Deep black-brown with beautiful head. Well-balanced flavor, very rich winter warmer. Give me more!"

"Caramel, butterscotch-sundae aroma. Rich, dark, creamy head. Sweet but not cloying flavor; light on grain. I enjoyed this brew; it was balanced, strong, inviting."

"Nice aroma. Good head and color. Full of flavor. Definitely a winter warmer in good balance."

ROSE'S RUSSIAN IMPERIAL STOUT WITH MAYO

Imperial Stout
First Place, Stout, 1992
Dick Van Dyke, Park Forest, Illinois
(grain/extract)

Ingredients for 5 gallons

5	pounds six-row English malt
6 2/3	pounds Northwestern dark malt extract
2	pounds 90 °L crystal malt
1	pound black patent malt
1	pound chocolate malt
1	pound Munich malt
1/4	pound wheat malt
1	ounce Chinook hops, 11.3 percent alpha acid (60 minutes)
5 1/2	ounces Eroica hops, 10.6 percent alpha acid (60 minutes)
1	ounce Kent Goldings hops, 4.7 percent alpha acid (45 minutes)
1	ounce Cascade hops, 4.9 percent alpha acid (45 minutes)
1	ounce Fuggles hops, 4.5 percent alpha acid (45 minutes)
1	ounce Chinook hops, 10.8 percent alpha acid (45 minutes)
1	ounce Kent Goldings hops, 4.7 percent alpha acid (30 minutes)
3/4	ounce Cascade hops, 4.9 percent alpha acid (30 minutes)
1	ounce Kent Goldings hops, 4.7 percent alpha acid (10 minutes)
1	ounce Fuggles hops, 3.4 percent alpha acid (10 minutes)
1	cup molasses
1	inch licorice stick
2	packages Red Star Champagne yeast
2/3	cup corn sugar to prime

Original specific gravity: 1.107
Final specific gravity: 1.047
Boiling time: 60 minutes
Primary fermentation: three days at 65 degrees F (18 degrees C) in plastic
Secondary fermentation: six days at 63 degrees F (17 degrees C) in glass
Tertiary fermentation: 28 days at 63 degrees F (17 degrees C) in glass
Age when judged (since bottling): six months

Brewer's specifics

Mash grains for 30 minutes at 130 degrees F (54 degrees C). Raise temperature to 150 degrees F (65 degrees C) for 60 minutes, then to 156 degrees F (69 degrees C) for 30 minutes.

Judges' comments

"Very good beer. Almost too much roasted flavor. Overcarbonated. Watch boiled grains for astringency. Very, very good."
"Molasses, licorice, roasted malt. Very nice beer. Well-made imperial stout."
"Rich, malty, fruity aroma. Alcohol evident in aroma. Thick, tight, compacted head. Good color and clarity. Very warming. Very smooth, drinkable beer. It leaves a warm feeling in my stomach."

BALTIC STOUT

Imperial Stout
Second Place, Stout, 1991
Wendell Choinsky, Germantown, New York
(grain/extract)

Ingredients for 3 1/2 gallons
9   pounds John Bull unhopped dark extract
1/2   pound roasted barley
1   pound pale malt
2   cups oatmeal
1/2   pound crystal malt
1   ounce Northern Brewer hops, 8 percent alpha acid
         (60 minutes)
1/2   ounce Cascade hops, 5.5 percent alpha acid
         (60 minutes)
1/2   ounce Cascade hops, 5.5 percent alpha acid
         (five minutes)
1/2   teaspoon gypsum
1   package Edme ale yeast
1   package Lalvin 1118 yeast
1/2   cup corn sugar to prime

Original specific gravity: 1.132
Final specific gravity: 1.052
Boiling time: 60 minutes
Primary fermentation: six days at 60 degrees F (15 degrees C) in plastic
Secondary fermentation: 21 days at 60 degrees F (15 degrees C) in glass
Age when judged (since bottling): 13 months

Brewer's specifics
Step infusion mash the grains and oatmeal for 90 minutes at 120 degrees F (49 degrees C), 150 degrees F (66 degrees C), and 158 degrees F (70 degrees C).

Judges' comments
"Some residual sweetness. Could be aided by the addition of more hops."
"Excellent beer. Could use more bittering hops."

NEW YEAR'S DAY

Dry Stout
Third Place, Stout, 1989
Paddy Giffen, Cotati, California
(all grain)

Ingredients for 5 gallons

5	pounds British pale malt
4	pounds Klages malt
1 1/2	pounds roasted barley
1	pound CaraPils malt
1	pound Vienna malt
1/2	pound wheat malt
1/2	pound 90 °L crystal malt
4	ounces chocolate malt
4	ounces black patent malt
1/4	ounce Chinook hop pellets (60 minutes)
1/4	ounce Northern Brewer hop pellets (60 minutes)
1	ounce Cascade hop pellets (30 minutes)
1/4	ounce Chinook hop pellets (30 minutes)
1	ounce Cascade hop pellets (dry)
	Brewer's Choice Chico liquid ale yeast
2/3	cup corn sugar for priming

Original specific gravity: 1.055
Final specific gravity: 1.017
Boiling time: 60 minutes
Primary fermentation: one week at 60 degrees F (15.5 degrees C) in glass
Secondary fermentation: two weeks at 60 degrees F (15.5 degrees C) in glass
Age when judged (since bottling): four months

Brewer's specifics

One-step infusion mash at 158 degrees F (70 degrees C). Steep grains, rack in 1 gallon of water. Steep to boil then sparge with 1 quart water at 170 degrees F (76.5 degrees C) and add to boil. Add 1 ounce of Cascade hops to the primary fermenter for aroma.

Judges' comments

"Malty aroma. Good rocky head, drops fairly quickly. Good roasted barley flavor; a little light in hop bitterness. A good beer. Well done!"
"Hop aroma — Cascade? Great stout head. Great flavor balance, but way too light. No defects. Overall it needs more flavor; more roasted barley and more kettle hops."

OAST HOUSE OATMEAL STOUT

Classic Dry Stout
Third Place, Stout, 1992
Paul Hale, East Northport, New York
(all grain)

Ingredients for 5 gallons

7	pounds two-row pale malt
1/2	pound two-row dextrin malt
1/2	pound two-row dark caramel malt
1	pound six-row roasted barley
1	pound flaked barley
1 1/8	pounds oatmeal
1	cup malted wheat
1 3/4	ounces Northern Brewer, 6.8 alpha acid (60 minutes)
	Wyeast No. 1056 yeast starter from previous batch
1/2	cup corn sugar for priming

Original specific gravity: 1.052
Final specific gravity: 1.014
Boiling time: 60 minutes
Primary fermentation: six days at 65 degrees F (18.5 degrees C) in glass
Secondary fermentation: four days at 65 degrees F (18.5 degrees C) in glass
Age when judged (since bottling): five months

Brewer's specifics

Mash grains for 20 minutes at 130 degrees F (54.5 degrees C). Raise to 155 degrees F (68.5 degrees C) for 60 minutes.

Judges' comments

"Excellent stout. A bit too sweet for dry. Finishes powdery from the astringency. Could use more roasted barley and less dark grains."
"Very good beer, but it could use more roasted barley flavor. Excellent flavor. Burnt bitterness is a little harsh."
"Coffeelike flavor is very evident. Very pleasant dry finish in the mouth. Just slightly too bitter in the finish."

New Stout II

Foreign-style
First Place, Stout, 1993
David and Melinda Brockington, Seattle, Washington
(all grain)

Ingredients for 5 gallons

9	pounds English pale malt
3	pounds roasted barley
1/2	pound 40 °L crystal malt
1/2	pound black patent malt
2	ounces Goldings hops (60 minutes)
	Wyeast No.1084 liquid yeast culture
3/4	cup corn sugar to prime

Original specific gravity: 1.060
Final specific gravity: 1.016
Boiling time: 60 minutes
Primary fermentation: 15 days at 65 degrees F (18 degrees C) in glass
Age when judged (since bottling): four months

Brewers' specifics

Mash grains at 155 degrees F (68 degrees C) for 60 minutes.

Judges' comments

"Roasted flavor not quite there. No strong off-flavors."
"Very good! Work on conditioning to fix the head."
"Malt evident, needs more hops. Slightly out of balance on the sweet side."
"Malty flavor. Perhaps just a little too sweet in the finish."

PART II

LAGER

Lagers are produced with bottom-fermenting *Saccharomyces uvarum* (or *carlsbergensis*) strains of yeast at colder fermentation temperatures than ales. This cooler environment reduces the natural production of esters and other fermentation byproducts, creating a cleaner-tasting product.

CHAPTER 9

BOCK

No one seems to know what Bock means. The literal translation is goat, but that makes little sense in a beer context. Some brewers believe that Bock is a corruption of Einbeck, the German town credited with the development of the style. Regardless, Bock beers are very malty and fairly high in alcohol. Lagering gives these beers an incredibly clean taste, free of fruity and estery yeast byproducts. A deep, chocolatey, candylike flavor characterizes the best examples, with just the right amount of hop bitterness to balance the delicious maltiness. Helles Bock makes use of lots of pale malt so roasty and caramelly flavors are not present. Lager these brews slowly, and be patient.

AHA National Homebrew Competition Style Guidelines
a) Traditional German Bock – Copper to dark brown. Full body. Malty sweet character predominates in aroma and flavor with some toasted chocolate. Low bitterness. Low hop flavor, "noble-type" OK. No hop aroma. No fruitiness or esters. Low to medium diacetyl OK.
b) Helles (light) Bock – Pale to amber. Other characters same as traditional German Bock without chocolate character. Medium to full body.
c) Doppelbock – Light to very dark; amber to dark brown. Very full body. Malty sweetness evident in aroma and flavor can be intense. High alcoholic flavor. Slight fruitiness and esters OK, but not very desirable. Low bitterness. Low hop flavor, "noble-type" OK. No hop aroma. Low diacetyl OK.

d) Eisbock – A stronger version of Doppelbock. Deep copper to black. Very alcoholic.

OG (Balling/Plato)	Percent alc./vol.	IBUs	SRM
a) Traditional German Bock			
1.066-74 (16.5-18.5)	6-7.5%	20-30	20-30
b) Helles (light) Bock			
1.066-68 (16.5-17)	6-7.5%	20-35	4.5-6
c) Doppelbock			
1.074-80 (18.5-20)	6.5-8%	17-27	12-30
d) Eisbock			
1.092-116 (23-29)	8.6-14.4%	26-33	18-50

DOPPELBOCK TWO

Doppelbock
First Place, Bock, 1991
Thomas Griffith, Franklin, Massachusetts
(grain/extract)

Ingredients for 5 gallons

15	pounds Laaglander dry light malt extract
8	ounces crystal malt
6	ounces chocolate malt
2	ounces Eroica hops (85 minutes)
1	ounce Tettnanger hops (10 minutes)
1	ounce Tettnanger hops (one minute)
1/2	teaspoon gypsum
1	teaspoon yeast energizer
1	teaspoon Irish moss (15 minutes)
	Wyeast No. 2206 liquid yeast
7/8	cup corn sugar to prime

Original specific gravity: 1.104
Final specific gravity: 1.051
Boiling time: 85 minutes
Primary fermentation: six weeks at 48 degrees F (9 degrees C) in glass
Secondary fermentation: eight weeks at 58 degrees F (14.5 degrees C) in glass
Age when judged (since bottling): 12 months

Brewer's specifics
Bring water to boil, steep grains for 30 minutes, then sparge with 2 quarts of 168-degree-F (75.5-degree-C) water.

Judges' comments
"Very alcoholic, malty aroma. Slightly salty finish, big malty sweetness, nice bitterness. Finish is slightly smoky-phenolic, roasty. Reduce salts, slight astringency from roast."
"Malty, good balance for style. What a great beer!"
"Nice malt sweetness, some bitterness, very long alcoholic finish. Fabulous!"

No Stupid Name

Helles Bock
Third Place, Bock, 1989
Peter Jelenik, Portland, Oregon
(all grain)

Ingredients for 5 gallons

11	pounds Klages malt
2	pounds German Munich malt
1	pound dextrin malt
1/3	pound crystal malt (boil)
1/2	ounce Hallertauer hops (finish)
2	teaspoons gypsum
	Wyeast No. 2042 liquid yeast

Original specific gravity: 1.067
Final specific gravity: 1.010
Boiling time: 90 minutes
Primary fermentation: four weeks at 55 degrees F (13 degrees C) in glass
Secondary fermentation: two months at 55 degrees F (13 degrees C) in glass
Age when judged (since bottling): 1 1/2 months

Brewer's specifics

Two-step mash at 120 and 156 degrees F (49 and 69 degrees C). Carbonated by natural kraeusen.

Judges' comments

"Very malty aroma with hint of DMS; otherwise clean. Color pretty much in line for a Helles, but leans toward Vienna. Could be more golden. Thin, retentive head with small-bubble beading. Very clear. Malty flavor, good balance, noticeable alcohol. Slightly fruity, sweet, full palate. A tad caramelly with a dryish finish — nice. Good example of style, just lacks some of the snap and finesse that comes from extended lagering."

"Good malt aroma, light hops, no off-odors. Good color and clarity; fair head retention. Malty sweet; some sweetness comes from a fruity character. Slight phenolic-bitter aftertaste. Perhaps tannins from oversparging?"

"Pleasant aroma. Very appealing appearance. Enjoyable flavor. Overall, I'm satisfied."

BASICALLY BOCK

Traditional German Bock
Second Place, Bock, 1990
Phil Rahn, St. Peters, Missouri
(all grain)

Ingredients for 5 gallons
10	pounds Klages malt
4	pounds Munich malt
2	pounds crystal malt
6	ounces chocolate malt
1	ounce Perle hops (60 minutes)
1 1/2	ounces Hallertauer hops (40 minutes)
1/2	ounce Hallertauer hops (finish)
	Wyeast No. 2308 Munich liquid yeast

Original specific gravity: 1.068
Final specific gravity: 1.026
Primary fermentation: two months at 44 degrees F (6.5 degrees C) in glass
Secondary fermentation: two months at 65 degrees F (18.5 degrees C) in glass
Age when judged (since bottling): three months

Brewer's specifics
Mash for two hours at 149 degrees F (65 degrees C). Forced CO_2 to carbonate.

Judges' comments
"Sweet, malty nose. Slight sourness. Very clear beer; dark, reddish-brown color is on the dark side of the Bock scale. Really nice creamy head. Malty-sweet flavor. Slightly mouth-drying middle with a sweet, hoppy finish. Noticeable alcohol; hops linger in the finish. Nicely made Bock. It tastes a bit too sweet and the hops linger a bit too long, but it's clean and very drinkable."

"Rich, malty bouquet with slightly smoky character. Faintly alcoholic. Appearance is very clean — filtered or transferred? Head retention is a little weak. Nice, clean brew. Full malt character holds throughout, nicely balanced by hops in mid-palate and finish. Slightly alcoholic and warming. Body appropriate for style; perhaps a touch thin. Overall, clean and nicely balanced. Dryness hangs on the palate a bit too long. It dances the line between bock and Doppelbock. Cut back on dark grain a bit."

"Malty aroma is as it should be. Very clear with red-orange tones. Nice medium, retentive head."

"Rich, malty palate; roasted malt flavor fairly well-balanced. Slightly harsh aftertaste. Full, rich body. Overall, a nice rendition of German Bock. It is slightly dark, a tad too well-hopped, and slightly overdone with roasted malt."

SCINTILLATOR

Doppelbock
First Place, Bock, 1992
Steve Dempsey, Fort Collins, Colorado
(grain/extract)

Ingredients for 5 gallons

7	pounds Munich malt
2	pounds 20 °L crystal malt
3 1/3	pounds BME Munich Gold malt extract
1	pound light dry malt extract
1 1/4	ounces Hallertauer hops, 4.1 percent alpha acid
1	ounce Tettnanger hops, 3.8 percent alpha acid
1/2	teaspoon salt
1/3	teaspoon gypsum
1 2/3	teaspoon chalk
1/3	teaspoon Epsom salts
	Wyeast No. 2308 liquid yeast

Original specific gravity: 1.080
Final specific gravity: 1.028
Primary fermentation: one day at 65 degrees F (18 degrees C) in glass
Secondary fermentation: 21 days at 47 degrees F (8 degrees C) in glass
Tertiary fermentation: 21 days at 38 degrees F (3 degrees C) in stainless steel
Age when judged (since bottling): 15 months

Brewer's specifics

Mash grains at 156 degrees F (69 degrees C) for 120 minutes.
Force carbonate in keg.

Judges' comments

"This beer has a lot of unfermented dextrines."
"I wish this beer had been better conditioned. It could have been excellent."
"I taste the malt and hop but believe a yeasty off-flavor affects the aftertaste."

Bock Aasswards

Doppelbock
First Place, Bock, 1990
Darryl Richman, Northridge, California
(all grain)

Ingredients for 15 gallons

24	pounds Munich malt
6	pounds Vienna malt
6	pounds Klages malt
1 1/2	pounds 80 °L crystal malt
7	ounces Hallertauer hops (180 minutes)
2/3	ounce calcium carbonate
	ML-1 liquid lager yeast
14	ounces dextrose for priming

Original specific gravity: 1.074
Final specific gravity: 1.022
Primary fermentation: four weeks at 48 degrees F (9 degrees C)
Secondary fermentation: six weeks at 33 degrees F (0.5 degrees C)
Age when judged (since bottling): 2 1/2 months

Brewer's specifics

Mash grains at 122 degrees F (50 degrees C) for 50 minutes, raise temperature to 136 degrees F (58 degrees C) for 30 minutes, to 149 degrees F (65 degrees C) for 40 minutes, to 160 degrees F (71 degrees C) for 90 minutes, and to 171 degrees F (77 degrees C) for 15 minutes.

Judges' comments

"Very sweet, malty flavor. Good balance. Nice bubbles. Smooth with a sweet aftertaste. Nice malty body. Very nice beer. Good malty body and flavor. Tastes strong."

"Nice perfumy, malt nose with some hops and alcohol evident. Darkish brown, but within the appropriate color range. Good clarity. Big tan head with active beading. Nice smooth balance between hops and malt. Good, subtle but strong alcohol kick. Smooth finish. Some huskiness and a lingering hop flavor. Clean and very drinkable. Very well balanced in malt, hops, and alcohol."

"Aroma has a slight alelike fruitiness with bananalike notes. Cooler fermentation needed. Deep copper color. Hazy from overcarbonation. Excellent head retention. Conditioning a bit high — it almost gushed. Excellent alcohol flavor. Good balance of bitter and sweet. Malty aftertaste. Your recipe is excellent — don't mess with it. Perfect body. Overall excellent maltiness. Only fault is overconditioning and the slight banana ester."

SUPER BOWL BOCK

Helles Bock
Third Place, Bock, 1993
Alan Barnes, Nashville, Tennessee
(all grain)

Ingredients for 5 gallons

9 1/2	pounds Klages malt
1/4	pound crystal malt
1/2	pound CaraPils malt
1	ounce Perle hops, 6.2 percent alpha acid (60 minutes)
1	ounce Saaz hops, 3.2 percent alpha acid (five minutes)
	Wyeast No. 2206 liquid yeast culture
1 1/2	cups dry malt extract to prime

Original specific gravity: 1.060
Final specific gravity: 1.010
Primary fermentation: 30 days at 58 degrees F (14 degrees C) in glass
Age when judged (since bottling): 17 months

Brewer's specifics

Mash grains for one hour at 154 degrees F (68 degrees C).

Judges' comments

"Slightly stale, slight diacetyl. Good color. Malt flavor could be more pronounced. You hit the style just great. This is a hard beer to fault."

"Perhaps slightly overcarbonated. Nice sweet malt dominates flavor. Hops balance malt nicely. Cut back on bottling sugar. Very nice beer."

"Nice malty feel. Good balance of malt and hops. A pleasant, drinkable beer with no serious flaws. Good brewing technique and control."

"Though a little thin, the beer has a very nice hop/malt balance. Well done."

"Good malt sweetness. Very clean, nice balance. Maybe just a bit dark."

CHAPTER 10

BAVARIAN/CONTINENTAL DARK

European dark beers are characterized by the elegant flavor of traditional lager malts. A malt sweetness, subtly balanced by hop bitterness, and a brief whiff of hop aroma will tell you that these brews are well lagered and have used high-quality ingredients to their best advantage. Use Munich and Vienna malts and a true continental yeast for the best results.

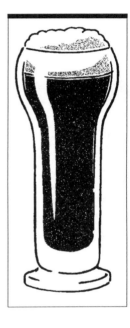

AHA National Homebrew Competition Style Guidelines

a) Munich Dunkel – Copper to dark brown. Medium body. Nutty, toasted, chocolatelike malty sweetness in aroma and flavor. Medium bitterness. Hop flavor and aroma, "noble-type" OK. No fruitiness or esters. Low diacetyl OK.

b) Schwarzbier – Dark brown to black. Medium body. Roasted malt evident. Low sweetness in aroma and flavor. Low to medium bitterness. Low bitterness from roast malt. Hop flavor and aroma, "noble-type" OK. No fruitiness, esters. Low diacetyl OK.

OG (Balling/Plato)	Percent alc./vol.	IBUs	SRM
a) Munich Dunkel			
1.052-56 (13-14)	4.5-5%	16-25	17-23
b) Schwarzbier			
1.044-52 (11-13)	3.8-5%	22-30	25-30

STU BREW

Munich Dunkel
First Place, Bavarian/Continental Dark, 1992
Stu Tallman, Rochester, Massachusetts
1992 Homebrewer of the Year
(all grain)

Ingredients for 10 gallons

15	pounds pale malt
4	pounds Munich malt
4	pounds 40 °L crystal malt
2 1/2	ounces Saaz hops (90 minutes)
	Wyeast No. 2026 liquid yeast

Original specific gravity: 1.060
Final specific gravity: 1.018
Boiling time: 90 minutes
Primary fermentation: 21 days at 50 degrees F (10 degrees C) in glass
Secondary fermentation: 21 days at 37 degrees F (3 degrees C) in glass
Age when judged (since bottling): four months

Brewer's specifics

Three-step upward infusion mash.

Judges' comments

"Slightly bitter start. Malty flavor. Sweet caramel finish. Very nice. Good balance. Clean."
"Very nice! Smooth malty taste. True to style and perfectly clean."
"Nice malty character. Smooth, a little sweet and caramelly. Good. Hops are good. Sulfury flavors come out as beer warms."

JAMIE BEER

Munich Dunkel
First Place, Bavarian/Continental Dark, 1991
Jim Post, Newtown, Connecticut
1991 Homebrewer of the Year
(grain/extract)

Ingredients for 5 gallons

12 1/2	pounds Munton and Fison pale two-row malt
2	pounds William's caramel malt
3	ounces William's dark dry Australian malt extract
3	ounces Mount Hood hops (60 minutes)
2	tablespoons calcium carbonate
2	tablespoons Irish moss
	New England Brewing Company lager yeast culture

Original specific gravity: 1.052
Final specific gravity: 1.012
Boiling time: 60 minutes
Primary fermentation: 24 days at 55 degrees F (13 degrees C) in glass
Age when judged (since bottling): two months

Brewer's specifics

Mash grains in a single-step infusion at 158 degrees F (70 degrees C) until conversion is complete.

Judges' comments

"Malty with chocolate flavor coming through. Well-balanced, a little watery. Very good brew, nice balance with malt."
"Aroma is nutty, malty, clean, balanced, and interesting — perfect! Well-balanced, full flavor, a little vegetal. Good nutty flavors, appropriate bitterness. A well-crafted beer, clean and almost perfect for style. A touch watery. Maybe needs a touch more chocolate malt."

LADY OF THE MORNING

Continental Dark
First Place, Bavarian/Continental Dark, 1989
Ross Herrold, La Porte, Indiana
(grain/extract)

Ingredients for 5 gallons

4	pounds Alexander's pale malt extract
2	pounds dark diastatic malt extract
1/2	pound crystal malt
1	ounce Hallertauer hops (60 minutes)
1/2	ounce Cascade hops (60 minutes)
1	ounce Hallertauer hops (30 minutes)
1/2	ounce Willamette hops (30 minutes)
1	ounce Hallertauer hops (one minute)
	Wyeast Pilsener liquid lager yeast
3/4	cup dextrose to prime

Original specific gravity: not given
Final specific gravity: 1.013
Boiling time: 60 minutes
Primary fermentation: seven weeks at 50 degrees F (10 degrees C) in glass
Secondary fermentation: six weeks at 30 to 40 degrees F (-1 to 4.5 degrees C) in glass
Age when judged (since bottling): four months

Brewer's specifics

Preboil top-up water and prechill.

Judges' comments

"Orange-pineapple aroma with hoppy backdrop. Perfect color; good clarity. Nice creamy head. Chocolate tones overtaken by gasiness. Aggressive carbonation. Nice creaminess."

"Lovely, balanced aroma (some yeast here). Excellent-looking beer. Dry flavor. Needs more of everything (especially malt). Clean, no fermentation flaws, just needs more."

"Slightly fruity aroma. Nice malt. Hops OK. Good appearance. Flavor slightly diacetyl, slightly fruity. Needs hops. Balance OK. Slightly sharp aftertaste fades fast. A good beer, but thin. Tastes a bit old and slightly fruity. Could call it continental dark dry."

DIVERSEY LAGER

Continental Dark
First Place, Bavarian/Continental Dark, 1990
Ray Daniels, Chicago, Illinois
(grain/extract)

Ingredients for 5 gallons

6	pounds Yellow Dog amber malt extract
1 1/2	pounds Munich malt
2	ounces black patent malt
2	ounces maltodextrin
1/2	ounce Saaz hops (60 minutes)
1	ounce Saaz hops (45 minutes)
1	ounce Saaz hops (15 minutes)
1/4	ounce Saaz hops (two minutes)
	Wyeast No. 2042 Danish Lager liquid yeast
3/4	cup corn sugar to prime

Original specific gravity: 1.054
Final specific gravity: 1.024
Primary fermentation: 14 days at 50 degrees F (10 degrees C) in plastic
Lagered: 60 days at 35 degrees F (1.5 degrees C) in plastic
Age when judged (since bottling): four months

Brewer's specifics

Mash Munich malt 60 minutes at 150 degrees F (65.5 degrees C). Boil black malt for 60 minutes.

Judges' comments

"Clean aroma. Wonderful effort. The best I've drunk in competition. I can't find fault with your beer."

"Very fruity hop aroma — a little too flowery. Good color, clear. Right amount of hop and malt flavors. Good body. I was pleasantly surprised with the flavor after the aroma of hops. Good job!"

"Aroma is just right for category. Moderate head retention. Flavor is very nice, very smooth and well balanced. Overall the best yet. A great example of a dark lager."

CROSSWAYS DUNKELBRAU

Munich Dunkel
Third Place, Bavarian/Continental Dark, 1993
Dennis Kinvig, Toronto, Ontario
(grain/extract)

Ingredients for 5 gallons

2 1/3	pounds Bierkeller unhopped dark malt extract
4	pounds Muntons Continental Lager hopped malt extract
20	ounces light dry malt extract
10	ounces wheat malt
1	pound Munich malt
1/4	ounce Hallertauer hops (30 minutes)
1/4	ounce Hallertauer hops (20 minutes)
1/2	ounce Hallertauer hops ('tea' at bottling)
	Wyeast No. 2308 German lager liquid yeast culture
4 1/3	ounces dextrose at bottling

Original specific gravity: 1.061
Final specific gravity: 1.014
Boiling time: 30 minutes
Primary fermentation: 14 days at 55 degrees F (13 degrees C) in glass
Age when judged (since bottling): 4 1/2 months

Brewer's specifics

Mash all grains. Boil 2 cups water with the dextrose to make the priming solution. Remove pot from heat and add the 1/2 ounce of Hallertauer hops. Strain the liquid into bottling bucket.

Judges' comments

"Lots of malt character, good amount of roasted malts. Too much bittering hops."
"A very good beer. Could be more complex. Reduce hoppiness."
"Medium to heavy hop flavor blends well with malt. Hopping may be a bit high for style."
"Could be more malty for amount of hops. Definite hop flavor. Very easy drinking beer with a bit too much hop finish. Good job."

CHAPTER 11

DORTMUND/EXPORT

A classic lager, Dortmunder beer is named for Dortmund, Germany, where it originated. These beers are highly attenuated, resulting in a sparkling, pale, dry brew with the traditional nose of "noble-type" hops like Hallertauer, Tettnanger, and Saaz. Dortmund has traditionally used extremely hard water, resulting in a sharp character that is unmistakable.

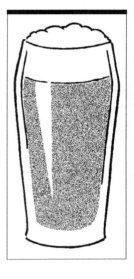

AHA National Homebrew Competition Style Guidelines

Pale to golden. Medium body. Medium malty sweetness. Medium bitterness. Hop flavor "noble-type" and aroma OK. No fruitiness, esters, or diacetyl. Alcoholic warmth evident.

OG (Balling/Plato)	Percent alc./vol.	IBUs	SRM
1.048-56 (12-14)	4.8-6%	23-29	4-6

REAGAN KNEW

Dortmund/Export
First Place, Dortmund/Export, 1989
Todd Hanson, Sheboygan, Wisconsin
(all grain)

Ingredients for 10 gallons

17	pounds Schreier two-row pale malt
1 1/3	pounds Munich malt
2/3	pound wheat malt
1/3	pound 40 °L caramel malt
3/8	ounce Northern Brewer hops (90 minutes)
1/2	ounce Hallertauer hops (60 minutes)
3/8	ounce Northern Brewer hops (60 minutes)
3/8	ounce Hallertauer hops (30 minutes)
3/8	ounce Tettnanger hops (30 minutes)
1/2	ounce Hallertauer hops (finish)
1/4	ounce Tettnanger hops (finish)
1/4	ounce Cascade hops (finish)
1	ounce gypsum (for 25 gallons soft water)
	Red Star lager yeast

Original specific gravity: 1.054
Final specific gravity: 1.022
Boiling time: 120 minutes
Primary fermentation: seven weeks at 52 degrees F (11 degrees C) in glass
Secondary fermentation: five weeks at 52 degrees F (11 degrees C) in glass
Age when judged (since bottling): two months

Brewer's specifics

Mash grains with a protein rest at 122 degrees F (50 degrees C) for 45 minutes, boost temperature to between 155 and 156 degrees F (68.5 and 69 degrees C) for 16 minutes, rest at 155 to 156 degrees F (68.5 to 69 degrees C) for 35 minutes, then raise temperature to 170 degrees F (77 degrees C) for eight minutes. Sparge two hours and 45 minutes, collect wort until runoff is 1.003 specific gravity.
Force CO_2 to carbonate.

Judges' comments

"Excellent hoppy aroma. Very good appearance. Minimal head retention. Good body, clean taste. Excellent aftertaste; seems to have an English hop aroma."
"Nice clean aroma. Appears filtered and clear. Tastes a little too much like an ale. Overall a very nice, well-made beer."
"Great clarity. Weak on head retention. Flavor on the sweet side, weak on hops. Smooth but not crisp enough. Very drinkable, very good."

COLBY'S EXPORT

Dortmund/Export
Second Place, Dortmund/Export, 1989
Rodney Howard, Oakley, California
(all grain)

Ingredients for 6 gallons

6 3/4	pounds pale malt
2	pounds Munich malt
1/4	pound wheat malt
3/4	ounce Saaz hops (60 minutes)
1 1/2	ounces Saaz hops (30 minutes)
3/4	ounce Saaz hops (15 minutes)
1	ounce Saaz hops (finish)
	Whitbread lager yeast

Original specific gravity: 1.054
Final specific gravity: not given
Boiling time: 60 minutes
Primary fermentation: two weeks at 55 degrees F (12.5 degrees C) in glass
Secondary fermentation: four weeks at 45 degrees F (7 degrees C) in glass
Age when judged (since bottling): two months

Brewer's specifics

Dough-in grains with 3 gallons 70-degree-F (21-degree-C) water for 20 minutes. Raise temperature to 122 degrees F (50 degrees C). Once temperature is achieved, immediately remove heaviest 40 percent of mash to mash kettle. Bring 40 percent mash to 158 degrees F (70 degrees C) and hold for 10 minutes. Increase to boiling and immediately add back to 122-degree-F (50-degree-C) mash. Raise temperature to 156 degrees F (69 degrees C). Hold for 15 minutes. Start testing for starch conversion. Once conversion is complete sparge with 172-degree-F (79-degree-C) water. Sparge until clear. Force CO_2 to carbonate.

Judges' comments

"Excellent malt nose. Good color, great flavor; could be slightly low in hops. This is a fabulous beer. I wish I had another."

"Nice aroma; good balance. Good color, clarity and head retention. Nice smooth, clean flavor. Very drinkable. Keep up the good work!"

"Aroma is appropriate for class. Very clear appearance, fair head retention. Very good flavor with a slight buttery aftertaste. Overall this beer is reminiscent of a commercial brew."

GRAIN-N-BEERIT

Dortmund/Export
First Place, Dortmund/Export, 1992
Norman Dickenson, Santa Rosa, California
(all grain)

Ingredients for 10 gallons

17	pounds two-row pale malt
2	pounds Munich malt
1	pound Vienna malt
1	pound dextrin malt
1	ounce Perle hops, 7.6 percent alpha acid (60 minutes)
1 1/4	ounce Saaz hops, 2.8 percent alpha acid (60 minutes)
2	ounces Tettnanger hops, 3.2 percent alpha acid (30 minutes)
1/2	ounce Perle hops, 7.6 percent alpha acid (10 minutes)
	Wyeast No. 2206 liquid yeast
1 1/2	cups corn sugar to prime

Original specific gravity: 1.050
Final specific gravity: not given
Boiling time: 60 minutes
Primary fermentation: 10 days at 52 degrees F (11 degrees C) in glass
Age when judged (since bottling): four months

Brewer's specifics

Mash grains at 149 degrees F (65 degrees C) for 50 minutes then raise temperature to 168 degrees F (75 degrees C) for 10 minutes.

Judges' comments

"Good balancing act sustained through finish. Malt character a bit milky; hops could be more assertive. Good job, though!"
"Some sweetness but seems nicely balanced. A little overcarbonated."
"I like this from the nose all the way to the aftertaste, but I think it is a little overcarbonated and fruity for the style. Could use more hardness. Overall a very good beer."
"Good malt flavor. Nice balance. Slightly overcarbonated. Good clean finish. Maybe just a touch sweet for style."

STU BREW

Dortmund/Export
Second Place, Dortmund/Export, 1991
Stu Tallman, Rochester, Massachusetts
(all grain)

Ingredients for 10 gallons

17	pounds two-row pale malt
2	pounds Munich malt
1	pound CaraPils malt
6	ounces crystal malt
1	ounce Perle hops (60 minutes)
3	ounces Saaz hops (30 minutes)
2	ounces Saaz hops (12 minutes)
1	ounce Tettnanger hops (12 minutes)
1/2	teaspoon gypsum
	Wyeast No. 2206 liquid yeast

Original specific gravity: 1.054
Final specific gravity: 1.018
Boiling time: 60 minutes
Primary fermentation: 14 days at 49 degrees F (9.5 degrees C) in metal
Secondary fermentation: 28 days at 49 degrees F (9.5 degrees C) in metal
Age when judged (since bottling): 3 1/2 months

Brewer's specifics

Mash grains at 120 degrees F (49 degrees C), raise temperature to 153 degrees F (67 degrees C), then to 165 degrees F (74 degrees C). Sparge with 175-degree-F (79.5-degree-C) water. Force CO_2 to carbonate.

Judges' comments

"Fairly pleasant to drink. A little harsh astringency. Some nice hop flavors here. Hop variety may be inappropriate. Pretty nice."
"Good beer. Cut back on bittering hops."

CHAPTER 12

MUNICH HELLES

Another classic European lager, Munich Helles is a celebration beer in many parts of Bavaria. It is mildly hopped and mildly malty, but has a fuller body than most lagers, which means some dextrin malts and not-so-attenuative yeasts can be used. As with all European lagers, you need to be patient and keep your Helles in cold storage for a while.

AHA National Homebrew Competition Style Guidelines
Pale to golden. Medium body. Medium malty sweetness. Low bitterness. Hop flavor and aroma "noble-type" OK. No fruitiness, esters. Low diacetyl OK.

OG (Balling/Plato)	Percent alc./vol.	IBUs	SRM
1.044-52 (11-13)	4.5-5.5%	18-25	3-5

MELTDOWN LAGER

Munich Helles
First Place, Munich Helles, 1992
Brian and Linda North, Franklin, Wisconsin
(grain/extract)

Ingredients for 5 1/2 gallons

5 1/2	pounds Munton and Fison pale dry malt extract
1/2	pound crystal malt
1/2	pound dextrin malt
1/2	ounce Hallertauer hops, 3.4 percent alpha acid (60 minutes)
1/2	ounce Hallertauer hops, 3.4 percent alpha acid (30 minutes)
1	ounce Saaz hops, 3 percent alpha acid (two minutes)
3/8	teaspoon gypsum
	Wyeast No. 2124 liquid yeast

Original specific gravity: 1.045
Final specific gravity: not given
Boiling time: 60 minutes
Primary fermentation: four days at 45 degrees F (7 degrees C) in glass
Secondary fermentation: 28 days at 35 degrees F (2 degrees C) in stainless steel
Age when judged (since bottling): six months

Judges' comments

"Fine example of Munich Helles. Could be higher in body and less carbonated. But not bad."
"Good beer. Cooler fermentation would help."
"Very fine effort. No real flaws. Good job."
"Very well-brewed beer. Noticeably better than others I have tasted."

HELLES

Munich Helles
Second Place, Munich Helles, 1989
David Miller, St. Louis, Missouri
(all grain)

Ingredients for 5 gallons

5 3/4	pounds two-row lager malt
1	pound CaraPils malt
1/4	pound 10 °L Munich malt
1 3/4	ounces Hallertauer hops (75 minutes)
1 3/4	ounces Hallertauer hops (45 minutes)
	Lactic acid (to acidify sparge water to pH 5.7)
	Wyeast No. 2007 St. Louis Lager liquid yeast
3/4	cup corn sugar to prime

Original specific gravity: 1.045
Final specific gravity: 1.013
Boiling time: 75 minutes
Primary fermentation: three weeks at 50 to 55 degrees F (10 to 13 degrees C) in glass
Secondary fermentation: one week at 50 to 55 degrees F (10 to 13 degrees C) in glass
Age when judged (since bottling): four months

Brewer's specifics

Mash grains with a protein rest 30 minutes at 131 degrees F (55 degrees C); starch rest 60 minutes at 149 to 155 degrees F (65 to 68.5 degrees C); mash-out five minutes at 168 degrees F (75.5 degrees C). Acidify sparge water to pH 5.7 with lactic acid. Sparge with 5 gallons water at 162 to 168 degrees F (72 to 75.5 degrees C).

Judges' comments

"Color is very light, almost yellow. Could use a more distinct hop flavor. Needs more carbonation; pleasant taste."

WHERE IN THE HELLES MUNICH?

Munich Helles
First Place, Munich Helles, 1991
Steven and Christina Daniel, League City, Texas
(all grain)

Ingredients for 5 gallons

8	pounds two-row malt
2	pounds light crystal malt
2	pounds Munich malt
1 1/4	ounces (25 IBU) Hallertauer hops (90 minutes)
	Wyeast No. 308 liquid yeast in homemade starter

Original specific gravity: 1.052
Final specific gravity: 1.015
Boiling time: 90 minutes
Primary fermentation: three weeks at 50 degrees F (10 degrees C) in stainless steel
Secondary fermentation: four weeks at 32 degrees F (0 degrees C) in stainless steel
Age when judged (since bottling): one month

Brewer's specifics

Mash grains at 151 degrees F (66 degrees C) for one hour.
Force carbonate in keg, counterpressure bottle.

Judges' comments

"Very prominent malty aroma, clean. Clean, characteristic taste with only slight oxidation. Bitterness prevails in the finish. Enough malt is present, maybe too much hops."

"Nice clean, malty nose. Body a bit thin."

"Maltiness jumped right out of the glass. Really good balance, nice sweet malt balance. A slight smokiness, a hint of oxidation. I really like this a lot!"

MUNICH HELLES

Munich Helles
First Place, Munich Helles, 1993
Donald J. Weaver, New Freedom, Pennsylvania
(all grain)

Ingredients for 5 gallons

3	pounds Klages malt
2 1/2	pounds lager malt
1 1/2	pounds Munich malt
1 1/2	pounds CaraPils malt
1 1/2	ounces Saaz hops, 3.1 percent alpha acid (45 minutes)
1/2	ounce Saaz hops, 3.1 percent alpha acid (20 minutes)
	Wyeast No. 2308 liquid yeast culture
3/4	cup corn sugar to prime

Original specific gravity: 1.045
Final specific gravity: 1.012
Boiling time: 90 minutes
Primary fermentation: 26 days at 42 to 60 degrees F (6 to 16 degrees C) in glass
Secondary fermentation: 16 days at 43 degrees F (6 degrees C) in glass
Age when judged (since bottling): four months

Brewer's specifics

Mash grains at 124 to 127 degrees F (51 to 53 degrees C) for 30 minutes. Raise to 147 to 155 degrees F (64 to 68 degrees C) for 60 minutes. Raise to 168 degrees F (76 degrees C) for five minutes. Sparge with 5 gallons of 168-degree-F (76-degree-C) water.

Judges' comments

"Sweetness is out of style. Warm fermentation qualities. Cool your fermentation down a bit, maybe change yeast."

"Very good flavor and balance. Pretty darn close to commercial examples of style. Seemed to have just a bit of a soapy aftertaste, oxidized?"

"Tasty malt character well-balanced with tingly conditioning. Sweetish at first but dries out in aftertaste."

"Nice maltiness, but fades too quick, astringent. Fusel-alcohols are objectionable. Nice drinkable beer."

CHAPTER 13

CLASSIC PILSENER

In one variation or another, Pilsener is one of the most popular beer styles in the world. Pilsener has its origins firmly rooted in the European lager tradition, which requires clean fermentations and an elegant hop character. Most good examples use exclusively Saaz hops for bitterness and aroma. Look for a spicy whiff of hops in the aroma, and a soft, caramelly sweetness in the flavor that is sheer beer heaven. Pilsener Urquell is the standard commercial comparison for this challenging brew.

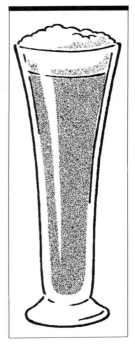

AHA National Homebrew Competition Style Guidelines
a) **German** – Pale to golden. Light to medium body. High hop bitterness. Medium "noble-type" hop flavor and aroma. Low maltiness in aroma and flavor. No fruitiness, esters. Very low diacetyl OK.
b) **Bohemian** – Pale to golden. Light to medium body. Medium to high bitterness. Low to medium "noble-type" hop flavor and aroma. Low to medium maltiness in aroma and flavor. No fruitiness, esters. Low diacetyl OK.

OG (Balling/Plato)	Percent alc./vol.	IBUs	SRM
a) German			
1.044-50 (11-12.5)	4-5%	30-40	2.5-4
b) Bohemian			
1.044-56 (11-14)	4-5%	35-45	3-5

BME PILSENER

Continental Pilsener
First Place, Pilsener, 1990
Sal Pennacchio, Staten Island, New York
(extract)

Ingredients for 5 gallons

6 2/3	pounds BME Munich Gold malt extract
1 1/4	ounces Hallertauer hops (45 minutes)
3/4	ounce Saaz hops (30 minutes)
1/2	ounce Saaz hops (two minutes)
1/4	ounce Saaz hops (dry)
1	pint M.eV. No. 001 German lager yeast

Original specific gravity: 1.048
Final specific gravity: 1.012
Primary fermentation: one week at 50 degrees F (10 degrees C) in glass
Secondary fermentation: two weeks at 35 to 40 degrees F (1.5 to 4.5 degrees C) in glass
Age when judged (since bottling): 3 1/2 months

Brewer's specifics

Force CO_2 to carbonate.

Judges' comments

"Aroma is very light. Good color, great head, crystal clear, very good. Finish is a little pronounced. Malt-hop balance is good. Good body. Very good beer."

"Faint aroma but no points off. Excellent color, good head, clear. Flavor a little dry and overcarbonated at the start. Nice malt, but could use a touch more hop kick. Good body. Very pleasant and drinkable. Clean, just a touch bland."

"Good spicy hop aroma. Mild malt aroma not perceptible. Yeast spiciness maybe from a temperamental yeast fermented at the wrong temperature. Nice tiny bubbles. Bitter aftertaste not appropriate. What type of hops are you using? Hops used are not the continental character. Overall a very nice beer. Look to improve yeast, hops, and fermentation temperature. What kind of yeast did you use? It might be the wrong yeast."

YELLOW DOGS PILSENER

Bohemian
First Place, Classic Pilsener, 1991
Matthew Holland, Park City, Utah
(extract)

Ingredients for 5 gallons

6	pounds William's American light malt extract
1	pound William's Australian light malt extract
1/2	ounce Chinook hops, 11.5 percent alpha acid (60 minutes)
1	ounce Saaz hops, 3.5 percent alpha acid (15 minutes)
1	ounce Saaz hops, 3.5 percent alpha acid (finish)
1	ounce Saaz hops, 3.5 percent alpha acid (dry)
1 1/2	teaspoons Irish moss (30 minutes)
	Wyeast Bohemian Lager liquid yeast
5/8	cup corn sugar to prime

Original specific gravity: 1.044
Final specific gravity: 1.011
Boiling time: 60 minutes
Primary fermentation: 14 days at 54 degrees F (12 degrees C) in plastic
Age when judged (since bottling): 2 1/2 months

Judges' comments

"Beautiful Saaz aroma. Slightly malty undertones, clean. Malty sweet with just the right amount of hops. Nice lingering aftertaste, great flavor. Good balance. Excellent, clean beer. No faults at all (which is hard to do in this category). A true classic."

"Very delicate malt-floral aroma. Fantastic malt flavor, could possibly be a bit more bitter. Nice bubbles, nice smooth taste. Subtle Pilsener flavors, great attention to detail. Excellent job!"

DISTINCTLY DEUTSCH PILSNER

German
First Place, Classic Pilsener, 1992
Patrick Drigans, Buffalo, Minnesota
(all grain)

Ingredients for 5 gallons

10	pounds German Pilsener malt
1	pound CaraPils malt
1	ounce Saaz hops, 3.6 percent alpha acid (60 minutes)
1	ounce Saaz hops, 3.6 percent alpha acid (35 minutes)
1	ounce Saaz hops, 3.6 percent alpha acid (20 minutes)
2	teaspoons yeast nutrient (20 minutes)
1	teaspoon Irish moss (20 minutes)
1	ounce Saaz hops, 3.6 percent alpha acid (two minutes)
1	ounce Saaz hops, 3.2 percent alpha acid (dry)
	Wyeast No. 2035 liquid yeast
3/4	cup corn sugar to prime
1	teaspoon ascorbic acid (in solution)

Original specific gravity: 1.045
Final specific gravity: 1.013
Boiling time: 90 minutes
Primary fermentation: 13 days at 68 degrees F (20 degrees C) in glass
Secondary fermentation: 14 days at 35 degrees F (2 degrees C) in glass
Age when judged (since bottling): six months

Brewer's specifics

Step infusion mash: 20 minutes at 113 degrees F (45 degrees C), and 15 minutes at 140 degrees F (60 degrees C). Hold at 154 degrees F (68 degrees C) until conversion. Raise temperature to 168 degrees F (75 degrees C) for 10 minutes. Sparge with 6 gallons 170-degree-F (77-degree-C) water. Gelatin finings added in secondary. One teaspoon ascorbic acid added at bottling.

Judges' comments

"Hopping right at the top end of range, malt needs to be up there, too. Clean fermentation."
"A good drinkable brew but a little heavy on the hops and could use more malt."
"The beer is not fully rounded, though it is well-made and has Pilsener attributes. A nice beer. A bit more malt and malt complexity would be nice."
"Balance toward hops. Very good beer."

PILSENER URPWELL

Continental Pilsener
Second Place, Pilsener, 1990
Quentin Smith, Rohnert Park, California
(all grain)

Ingredients for 6 gallons

10	pounds Klages malt
1/4	ounce Chinook hops (60 minutes)
3/4	ounce Saaz hops (60 minutes)
1	teaspoon Irish moss (45 minutes)
1 1/2	ounces Saaz hops (30 minutes)
3/4	ounce Saaz hops (finish)
	Wyeast Bohemian liquid yeast
1 1/4	cups corn sugar to prime

Original specific gravity: 1.049
Final specific gravity: 1.013
Boiling time: 60 minutes
Primary fermentation: eight days at 56 degrees F (13.5 degrees C) in glass
Secondary fermentation: 10 days at 56 degrees F (13.5 degrees C) in glass, then 20 days at 32 degrees F (0 degrees C) in glass
Age when judged (since bottling): one month

Brewer's specifics

Mash 1 1/2 hours at 152 degrees F (66.5 degrees C). Sparge with soft water at 170 degrees F (76.5 degrees C).

Judges' comments

"Citrus-grapefruit aroma. Hops barely perceptible, malt not perceptible. Good effort for a difficult style. Try some quality European hops in the secondary fermenter and increase malt for more body."

"There is too much dryness, you could up the malt. Could be a little more bitter. Floral aftertaste. Very tasty beer, though a little thin."

"Nice spicy hop aroma, nice head formation, color, and clarity. Good body, nice mouthfeel. Very good effort, I like it. Nice balance of malt, clean."

"A floral hop aroma — fresh and clean. Nice hops in flavor, though very dry. Needs more malt to balance. Astringency in aftertaste. A pleasant, drinkable beer, but too light and dry for style. A clean, well-made refreshing summer beer."

OASIS LAGER

American Pilsener
First Place, Pilsener, 1989
Eric McClary, Carson City, Nevada
(all grain)

Ingredients for 5 gallons

6	pounds six-row lager malt
1/2	pound toasted six-row lager malt
1/2	ounce Saaz hop pellets (60 minutes)
1/4	ounce Saaz hop pellets (30 minutes)
1/4	ounce Saaz hop pellets (finish)
1 1/2	pounds long-grain rice, ground and gelatinized*
	Wyeast No. 2035 New Ulm lager yeast
1	teaspoon gelatin finings
1	cup dextrose to prime

Original specific gravity: 1.045
Final specific gravity: 1.011
Boiling time: 60 minutes
Primary fermentation: 3 1/2 weeks at 55 degrees F (13 degrees C) in glass
Secondary fermentation: two weeks at 55 degrees F (13 degrees C) in glass
Age when judged (since bottling): three months

Brewer's specifics

*Cook rice to gelatinize it. As the dried grains soak up water as they are heated, the solid starches become a gel. Cooking (boiling) explodes the starches so some of the sugars are accessible to the enzymes.

Toast malt by heating five minutes at 350 degrees F (176.5 degrees C).

Modified decoction mash: Mash-in at 120 degrees F (49 degrees C) for 45 minutes; add rice cooked in 1 1/2 gallons water to raise mash temperature to 135 degrees F (57 degrees C); add 1 1/2 gallons boiling water to raise temperature to 149 degrees F (65 degrees C) over 30-minute period. Hold temperature for 45 minutes until conversion. Sparge with 170-degree-F (76.5-degree-C) water. Finishing hops steeped for 15 minutes after boil. Gelatin finings added last five days of ferment.

Judges' comments

"Fine aroma. Very nice appearance, very clear; thick head. Slight astringency, but should fall out in short amount of time. Bitter aftertaste. Overall a very good beer."

"Good color, good clarity. Excessive head. Hop flavor appropriately light. Extremely carbonated, even for class. Aftertaste too hoppy."

"Slightly skunky-hoppy. Slight haze. Color and head OK. Clean taste with a good hop balance. Skunkiness went away after awhile."

CHAPTER 14

AMERICAN LAGER/CREAM ALE

More American-style lager is produced and consumed in the world than any other style of beer. Period. Among homebrewers it is considered one of, if not the most, difficult beers to brew. Incredibly pale in color, light in body, American light lager is a true test of clean fermentation techniques, subtle hopping schedules, and true lagering. Sometimes these beers are brewed at a slightly higher gravity, then diluted with water to achieve the light-bodied, pale beer. It is difficult to brew these beers from extract because of the light color required in the end product, and extracts often darken in the can as they get older. Corn and rice are often used to produce a crisp, refreshing flavor. With the addition of some coloring malts, American dark can be produced. You can get a Cream Ale by allowing your yeast to produce some fruity and estery flavors.

AHA National Homebrew Competition Style Guidelines
a) **Diet/Lite** – Very pale. Light body. Very low bitterness. No malt aroma or flavor. No hop aroma or flavor. Effervescent. No fruitiness, esters, or diacetyl.
b) **American Standard** – Very pale. Light body. Very low bitterness. Low malt aroma and flavor. Low hop aroma and flavor OK. Effervescent. No fruitiness, esters, or diacetyl.
c) **American Premium** – Very pale to golden. Light body. Low to medium bitterness. Low malt aroma and flavor OK. Low hop flavor or aroma OK.

Effervescent. No fruitiness, esters, or diacetyl.
d) Dry – Pale to golden. Light body. Low to medium bitterness. Low malt aroma or flavor. Low hop aroma and flavor. Effervescent. No fruitiness, esters, or diacetyl. No lingering aftertaste or bitterness.
e) Cream Ale/Lager – Very pale. Effervescent. Light body. Low to medium bitterness. Low hop flavor or aroma OK. Low fruitiness/ester OK. Can use ale or lager yeasts or combination of both.
f) American Dark – Deep copper to dark brown. Light to medium body. Low bitterness. Low malt aroma or flavor OK. Low hop flavor or aroma OK. Effervescent. No fruitiness, esters. Very low diacetyl OK.

OG (Balling/Plato)	Percent alc./vol.	IBUs	SRM
a) Diet/Lite			
1.024-40 (6-10)	2.9-4.2%	8-15	2-4
b) American Standard			
1.040-46 (10-11.5)	3.8-4.5%	5-17	2-4
c) American Premium			
1.046-50 (11.5-12.5)	4.3-5%	13-23	2-8
d) Dry			
1.040-50 (10-12.5)	4-5%	15-23	2-4
e) Cream Ale/Lager			
1.044-55 (11-14)	4.5-7%	10-22	2-4
f) American Dark			
1.040-50 (10-12.5)	4-5.5%	14-20	10-20

COLBY'S CREAM ALE

Cream Ale
First Place, American Lager/Cream Ale, 1989
Rodney Howard, Oakley, California
(all grain)

Ingredients for 6 gallons

8 1/2	pounds pale malt
1/2	pound Munich malt
1/2	pound flaked rice
1/3	ounce Eroica hop pellets (60 minutes)
1/3	ounce Eroica hop pellets (45 minutes)
1/3	ounce Galena hop pellets (30 minutes)
1/3	ounce Galena hop pellets (15 minutes)
1	ounce Fuggles hops (finish)
1	ounce Tettnanger hops (dry)
1	packet Whitbread lager yeast

Original specific gravity: 1.050
Final specific gravity: not given
Boiling time: 60 minutes
Primary fermentation: four weeks at 70 degrees F (21 degrees C) in glass
Secondary fermentation: three weeks at 45 degrees F (7.2 degrees C) in glass
Age when judged (since bottling): five months

Brewer's specifics

Heat water to 156 degrees F (69 degrees C). Add grains. Reheat to 156 degrees F (69 degrees C) and hold for 45 minutes. Start testing for starch conversion after 15 minutes. Once conversion is complete sparge with 172-degree-F (78-degree-C) water. Ferment at 65 degrees F (18.5 degrees C). Begin secondary fermentation at 50 degrees F (10 degrees C), drop the temperature no more than 5 degrees F (3 degrees C) per day. Age at 41 degrees F (5 degrees C) for three weeks. Force CO_2 to carbonate.

Judges' comments

"Clean, light, fruity nose. Dense fine head, full bead, distinct haze. Malty and corny character, appropriate light hoppy aftertaste. Slight astringency. Very close to Genesee! Excellent."

"Corny aroma, slight medicinal character. Yellow color, slight haze, good head. Corny start with a slightly malty finish. Good hop balance. Good example of a cream ale, good balance, clean finish."

"Lightly fruity aroma; innocuous aroma typical for style; no off-aromas noted. Creamy white head; good clarity and color; nice beading. Fruity-hoppy flavor; slightly sour and bitter in the finish; light body; full carbonation. This is a very good ale. The appearance is excellent. The beer is slightly overhopped and the finish is a little sour, marring what would otherwise be excellent."

PRE-PROHIBITION LAGER À LA GEORGE FIX

American Premium
First Place, American Lager/Cream Ale, 1991
Vern Wolff, Esparto, California
(all grain)

Ingredients for 10 gallons

7	pounds two-row pale malt
7	pounds six-row pale malt
7	pounds rolled barley
2	ounces homegrown Cluster hops (60 minutes)
1	ounce homegrown Cascade hops (five minutes)
	Butterfield Brewing Company liquid yeast culture in starter
1 1/2	cups dextrose to prime

Original specific gravity: 1.045
Final specific gravity: 1.011
Boiling time: 60 minutes
Primary fermentation: 16 days at 55 degrees F (13 degrees C) in glass
Age when judged (since bottling): three months

Brewer's specifics

Mash grains in a step infusion. First rest at 127 degrees F (53 degrees C) for 30 minutes. Raise temperature to 135 degrees F (57 degrees C) and hold for 30 minutes. Last rest at 147 degrees F (64 degrees C) for 30 minutes.

Judges' comments

"Aroma is almost neutral — good and clean. Great crisp clean flavor with medium malt and hop impact. Very good profile, though beer has too much flavor for style. Great brew except for the haze. Good job, a bit full, though."
"Balanced flavor, though slightly too much malt. Body slightly too full. Nicely made beer — a bit too much for style, but lovely!"

ARLINGTON ALE NO. 33

Cream Ale
First Place, American Lager/Cream Ale, 1990
Richard Schmit, Arlington Heights, Illinois
(grain/extract)

Ingredients for 5 gallons

3 1/3	pounds John Bull light hopped malt extract
2	pounds light dry malt extract
4	ounces toasted pale malt
3	ounces crystal malt
1/4	ounce Cascade hops (10 minutes)
1/4	ounce Willamette hops (10 minutes)
1/4	ounce Cascade hops (two minutes)
1/4	ounce Willamette hops (two minutes)
1	teaspoon Irish moss
1	teaspoon ascorbic acid
	Wyeast No. 1056 American ale liquid yeast
3/4	cup corn sugar for priming

Original specific gravity: 1.042
Final specific gravity: 1.013
Primary fermentation: eight days at 65 degrees F (18.5 degrees C) in plastic
Secondary fermentation: two days at 65 degrees F (18.5 degrees C) in plastic
Age when judged (since bottling): 6 1/2 months

Brewer's specifics

Steep grains, bring temperature to 200 degrees F (93.5 degrees C) and sparge. Add hops at end of boil.

Judges' comments

"Fruity bouquet. Good color and clarity. Nice flavor balance and aftertaste. Appropriate body for style. Very flavorful and enjoyable!"

"Aroma is clean, fresh and faintly malty with pleasant background hops. Cream ale looking. Flavor is really nice, well-balanced. The head was a bit too creamy; otherwise a fine, delicate brew with superb balance."

"Slight phenolic aroma. Faint, sweet malt nose; no hops. Great head, fine beading. A little dark for category. Very slight haze. Very good balance; just a tad sweet. Very slight astringency. Wonderfully creamy! The tingle of the fine bead on the tongue is delightful."

BUTT-SCRATCHER

American Premium
First Place, American Lager/Cream Ale, 1992
Steve and Christina Daniel League City, Texas
(all grain)

Ingredients for 5 gallons

3   pounds six-row malt
4   pounds two-row malt
1   pound rice
18   total IBUs, half Hallertauer, half Cascade hops
      Wyeast No. 2308 liquid yeast

Original specific gravity: 1.049
Final specific gravity: not given
Boiling time: 60 minutes
Primary fermentation: 21 days at 50 degrees F (10 degrees C) in stainless steel
Secondary fermentation: 30 days at 32 degrees F (0 degrees C) in stainless steel

Brewers' specifics

Precook rice prior to mash. Mash grains at 151 degrees F (66 degrees C) for 60 minutes.

Judges' comments

"Somewhat oxidized. Chalky in aftertaste. Watch oxygen pickup, otherwise a nice, clean, balanced taste."
"A good beer slightly marred by oxidation."
"Very smooth, nice maltiness (a bit too much, but still fine). Very slight tang."
"This is a fine beer overall. Has a nice warm alcohol presence. I like this one!"

LEAGUE CITY DARK

American Dark
Second Place, American Lager/Cream Ale, 1993
Steven and Christina Daniel, League City, Texas
(all grain)

Ingredients for 5 gallons

4	pounds domestic six-row malt
3	pounds Harrington two-row malt
1	pound cooked rice
2	ounces chocolate malt
1	pound dark crystal malt
1	ounce Cascade hops, 6.7 percent alpha acid (90 minutes)

Original specific gravity: 1.048
Final specific gravity: 1.012
Boiling time: 90 minutes
Primary fermentation: 14 days at 50 degrees F (10 degrees C) in stainless steel
Secondary fermentation: 30 days at 32 degrees F (0 degrees C) in stainless steel
Age when judged (since bottling): not given

Brewers' specifics

Mash grains for 90 minutes at 150 degrees F (66 degrees C). Force carbonate.

Judges' comments

"Sweetish, malty character predominates, nicely offset by roasted grain. Smooth, well-balanced effort. Just a touch more hops might help. A little hefty for an American Dark."

"Caramel flavor dominates — perhaps a bit too strong. Too rich. More rice or corn adjunct would bring this back. Lighten the crystal malt a bit."

"Rich, smooth, malty. Really a bit big for style but very tasty. I love this beer, but it is more in the style of a Munich Dunkel. Body a bit full for style."

CHAPTER 15

VIENNA/OKTOBERFEST/MÄRZEN

A wonderful caramelly sweetness characterizes these festival beers. Typically these beers are somewhat high in alcohol and deep copper in color. Brewed in the spring, lagered in caves for the summer, and served in October, Märzen and Oktoberfest were traditionally consumed at the world famous Oktoberfest in Munich.

Viennas are somewhat lower in alcohol than Oktoberfests and Märzens, and a little bit lighter at their maximum color. Careful conditioning, which produces a beautiful head and small bubbles, is also an attribute of these brews.

AHA National Homebrew Competition Style Guidelines

a) **Vienna** – Amber to deep copper/light brown. Toasted malt aroma and flavor. Low malt sweetness. Light to medium body. "Noble-type" hop bitterness low to medium. Low hop flavor and aroma, "noble-type" OK. No fruitiness, esters. Low diacetyl OK.

b) **Märzen/Oktoberfest** – Amber to deep copper/orange. Malty sweetness, toasted malt aroma and flavor dominant. Medium body. Low to medium bitterness. Low hop flavor and aroma, "noble-type" OK. No fruitiness, esters, or diacetyl.

OG (Balling/Plato)	Percent alc./vol.	IBUs	SRM
a) Vienna			
1.048-55 (12-13.5)	4.4-6%	22-28	8-12
b) Märzen/Oktoberfest			
1.052-64 (13-16)	4.8-6.5%	22-28	7-14

Beer Unnamed

Oktoberfest/Märzen
First Place, Vienna/Oktoberfest/Märzen, 1991
Dennis and Cindy Arvidson, Encinitas, Califorina
(all grain)

Ingredients for 15 gallons

15 1/2	pounds two-row malt
9	pounds Munich malt
2	pounds home-roasted two-row malt
1 1/2	pounds wheat malt
1	pound Scottish malt
1/4	pound roasted barley
3 1/4	ounces Styrian Goldings hops, 3 percent alpha acid (120 minutes)
2 1/2	ounces Saaz hops, 2.4 percent alpha acid (120 minutes)
3 1/6	grams calcium chloride in mash
3 1/6	grams calcium chloride in sparge
	Wyeast No. 2308 liquid lager yeast
3/4	cup corn sugar to prime

Original specific gravity: 1.060
Final specific gravity: 1.015
Boiling time: 120 minutes
Primary fermentation: 40 days at 38 degrees F (3.5 degrees C) in plastic
Secondary fermentation: 30 days at 38 degrees F (3.5 degrees C)
Age when judged (since bottling): eight months

Brewers' specifics

Mash grains 90 minutes at 156 degrees F (69 degrees C).

Judges' comments

"Nice malt, slight diacetyl and DMS. Good toasted aroma, nice hops. Good color, nice toasted malt flavor. Good balance and finish, slight oxidation. A great beer!"

"Nice toasted malt nose. Maltiness comes through nicely, followed by warming alcohol taste. Great-tasting beer, maybe a bit alcoholic for style and a tad cloudy."

"Toasted malt aroma, no hop aroma. Not much toasted flavor. Malt is there, some hop bitterness. Balance is OK, minimal aftertaste. Very good beer, needs more toasted flavor."

DOES EK KI?

Vienna
First Place, Vienna/Oktoberfest/Märzen, 1989
Charlie Olchowski, Greenfield, Massachusetts
(all grain)

Ingredients for 7 gallons

6 1/4	pounds Munton and Fison lager malt
5	pounds Ireks Munich malt
1 1/2	pounds Munton and Fison CaraPils malt
1	pound Munton and Fison crystal malt
1/2	pound Ireks Vienna malt
1 3/4	ounces Tettnanger hops (boil)
3/4	ounce Hallertauer hops (boil)
3/4	ounces Tettnanger hops (finish)
3/8	ounce Hallertauer hops (finish)
	Wyeast No. 2308 liquid yeast
3/4	cup corn sugar syrup

Original specific gravity: 1.052
Final specific gravity: 1.012
Boiling time: 90 minutes
Primary fermentation: 15 weeks at 33 to 48 degrees F (0.5 to 9 degrees C) in glass
Secondary fermentation: 14 weeks at 33 degrees F (0.5 degrees C) in glass
Age when judged (since bottling): eight months

Brewer's specifics

Two-step upward infusion mash. Raise temperature to 122 degrees F (50 degrees C), hold for one hour. Raise temperature to 154 degrees F (68 degrees C), hold for one hour.

Judges' comments

"Malty nose. Good color. Sweet malty flavor, finishes smooth. A very good beer. Slightly sweet."

"Nutty aroma which is not the true 'Munich malt' aroma. Appearance is A-1. Sweet but well-balanced for category. Overall a fine beer. Aroma and overcarbonation are the only problems."

"Malty aroma. A bit overcarbonated at opening. Malty sweet flavor, could use more bitterness to help balance it out. Nice malty sweetness yet a bit overpoweringly sweet."

LES DAMES DE PARIS

Vienna
First Place, Vienna/Oktoberfest/Märzen, 1990
Ron Page, Middletown, Connecticut
(all grain)

Ingredients for 13 gallons

15	pounds two-row malt
10	pounds pale ale malt
6	pounds Munich malt
1 1/2	pounds crystal malt
1	pound dextrin malt
2	ounces chocolate malt
3	ounces Hallertauer hops (60 minutes)
1	ounce Saaz hops (60 minutes)
1	ounce Tettnanger hops (60 minutes)
1/3	ounce Hallertauer hops (finish)
1/3	ounce Saaz hops (finish)
1/3	ounce Tettnanger hops (finish)
	Wyeast No. 2308 Munich lager liquid yeast

Original specific gravity: 1.055
Final specific gravity: 1.018
Primary fermentation: 20 days at 52 degrees F (11 degrees C) in glass
Secondary fermentation: seven weeks at 40 degrees F (4.5 degrees C) in glass
Age when judged (since bottling): 2 1/2 months

Brewer's specifics

Mash grains at 123 degrees F (50.5 degrees C) for 20 minutes. Raise temperature to 154 degrees F (68 degrees C) for 45 minutes, then to 158 degrees F (70 degrees C) for 45 minutes. Force CO_2 to carbonate.

Judges' comments

"Nice intense malty aroma, good balance. Good color, nice head. Nice malty sweetness comes through very well in the flavor. A tad sweet but OK for style. Could have more alcohol. Good body. Overall a very good Vienna. I could drink this all day!"
"Very nice malt aroma. Appearance almost perfect. Tastes almost like a commercial beer. Well balanced and smooth, malty. I could drink this all night."
"The head would not stand up at pour or when swirled in the glass. The flavor is right on! The hops are nice, but I could use a bit more. Outstanding beer! Gimme more!"

VIENNA LAGER

Vienna
First Place, Vienna/Oktoberfest/Märzen, 1992
Keith Weerts, Windsor, California
(grain/extract)

Ingredients for 5 gallons
4	pounds light malt extract
3	pounds Munich malt
2	pounds Vienna malt
1 1/2	pounds Klages malt
1/2	pound dextrin malt
2	ounces chocolate malt
1/2	ounce Saaz hops, 2.8 percent alpha acid (60 minutes)
1 1/2	ounce Saaz hops, 2.8 percent alpha acid (30 minutes)
1/2	ounce Saaz hops, 2.8 percent alpha acid (finish)
	Wyeast No. 2206 liquid yeast

Original specific gravity: 1.052
Final specific gravity: 1.012
Boiling time: 60 minutes
Primary fermentation: 11 days at 50 degrees F (10 degrees C) in plastic
Secondary fermentation: 10 days at 40 degrees F (4 degrees C) in glass
Tertiary fermentation: 20 days at 32 degrees F (0 degrees C) in glass
Age when judged (since bottling): nine months

Brewer's specifics
Mash grains at 152 degrees F (66 degrees C) for 60 minutes.

Judges' comments
"Wonderful beer. A little malt heavy for Vienna. Cut the malt about 10 percent and you have a winner."
"I like this Vienna. No off-flavors, clean. I could drink lots of this stuff."
"Good maltiness, very clean. Overall this is a bigger beer than expected — it's pushing the upper end of Vienna in all characteristics. Really excellent."

DOMINION DAY OKTOBERFEST

Märzen/Oktoberfest
First Place, Vienna/Oktoberfest/Märzen, 1993
John E. Janowiak, Adelphi, Maryland
(grain/extract)

Ingredients for 5 gallons

6 2/3	*pounds Bierkeller malt extract syrup*
1	*pound amber dry malt extract*
1/2	*pound 10 °L crystal malt*
1/2	*cup chocolate malt*
1	*ounce Cascade hops, 5.5 percent alpha acid (60 minutes)*
1	*ounce Hallertauer hops, 4.5 percent alpha acid (30 minutes)*
3/4	*ounce Tettnanger hops (one minute)*
	Wyeast No. 2206 liquid yeast culture
1/2	*cup corn sugar to prime*

Original specific gravity: 1.047
Final specific gravity: 1.014
Boiling time: 60 minutes
Primary fermentation: 11 days at 45 to 50 degrees F (7 to 10 degrees C) in glass
Secondary fermentation: 10 days at 45 to 50 degrees F (7 to 10 degrees C) in glass
Tertiary fermentation: 15 days at 35 to 40 degrees F (2 to 4 degrees C) in glass
Age when judged (since bottling): 11 months

Brewer's specifics
Steep grains until water begins to boil, then remove grains.

Judges' comments
"Clean maltiness, low hop bitterness, low hop flavor. Could use a touch more malt grainy character. Keep an eye on fermentation temperatures to prevent esters."
"Some fruitiness/esters. Very good beer. Could be a bit maltier."
"Clean. Malt flavors on subdued side. Hop level appropriate. Excellent beer."
"Good beer, nice balance. Seems to be missing a lot of lager character."

PART III

MIXED STYLE

Mixed-style beers are fermented or aged with
mixed traditions and can be brewed as ales or
lagers. Beers flavored with various herbs and spices
or classic styles that, for one reason or another,
resist being placed exactly within a given category
are called mixed-style beers.

CHAPTER 16

GERMAN-STYLE ALE

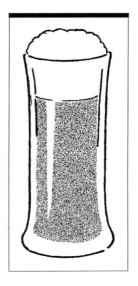

Altbier and Kölsch are somewhat mysterious beers. Characterized by hop spiciness and distinctive yeast characteristics, both styles can use wheat in the grist. Genuine Kölsch yeast is hard to find in the United States, but you may substitute an alt yeast instead. These beers are fermented warm, but aged cold. Use good, fresh "noble-type" hops and German malts. When you brew them right, these are truly unique and wonderfully refreshing beers.

AHA National Homebrew Competition Style Guidelines
a) Düsseldorf-style Altbier – Copper to dark brown. Medium to high bitterness. Very low hop flavor. No hop aroma. Light to medium body. Low fruitiness and esters. Traditionally fermented warm but aged at cold temperatures. Very low diacetyl OK.
b) Kölsch – Pale Gold. Low hop flavor and aroma. Medium bitterness. Light to medium body. Slightly dry, winy palate. Malted wheat OK. Lager or ale yeast or combination of yeasts OK.

OG (Balling/Plato)	Percent alc./vol.	IBUs	SRM
a) Düsseldorf-style Altbier			
1.044-48 (11-12)	4.3-5%	25-35	11-19
b) Kölsch			
1.042-46 (10.5-11.5)	4.4-5%	20-30	3.5-5

KÖLSCH

Kölsch
First Place, German-style Ale, 1990
Norman Dickenson, Santa Rosa, California
(all grain)

Ingredients for 5 gallons

9	pounds Klages two-row malt
1	pound wheat malt
4	ounces 20 °L crystal malt
2	ounces CaraPils malt
1	teaspoon gypsum
1/4	ounce Perle hop pellets (60 minutes)
1/4	ounce Saaz hop pellets (60 minutes)
1/2	ounce Tettnanger hop pellets (30 minutes)
1/2	ounce Hallertauer hop pellets (five minutes)
1/2	ounce Hallertauer hop pellets (dry)
	Wyeast No. 1338 Altbier liquid yeast
3/4	cup corn sugar for priming

Original specific gravity: 1.050
Final specific gravity: 1.018
Primary fermentation: eight days at 68 degrees F (20 degrees C) in glass
Secondary fermentation: four days at 55 degrees F (12 degrees C) in glass
Age when judged (since bottling): 3 1/2 months

Brewer's specifics
Mash 60 minutes at 156 degrees F (69 degrees C).

Judges' comments
"Malty aroma. Clear, gold color; excellent head retention. Good malt to hop balance. Well conditioned (maybe too well). Appropriate body. Very good beer. Dry palate. A little sweet."

"Very clean, light, fruity nose up front. Bouquet stays light. Very high, fine white head. Golden, light haze, fine bead. Malty tone with balanced hop aftertaste. Light balance of ingredients for true Kölsch. Body appropriate for style. Good mouthfeel. Very good brewing effort for a difficult style. High head and haze cost points."

"Malty with slight hop aroma. Fresh and clean. Dark golden; almost clear. Head too big, but it holds well. Nice lingering aftertaste; nice mouthfeel. Nice little, long-lasting bubbles. Overall a nice, neutral, fresh, pleasant beer."

KINSMAN JUNCTION KÖLSCH

Kölsch
Second Place, German-style Ale, 1991
Marlene Spears, Woburn, Massachusetts
(all grain)

Ingredients for 5 1/4 gallons

7 1/2	pounds Klages malt
1	pound Vienna malt
1/2	pound wheat malt
1	ounce Hersbrucker hops, 4 percent alpha acid (60 minutes)
1/4	ounce Saaz hops, 3 percent alpha acid (40 minutes)
1/2	ounce Fuggles hops, 4.2 percent alpha acid (40 minutes)
1/2	ounce Fuggles hops, 4.2 percent alpha acid (20 minutes)
1/2	ounce Saaz hops, 3 percent alpha acid (one minute)
1/4	ounce Saaz hops, 3 percent alpha acid (dry)
1	teaspoon Irish moss (10 minutes)
1	teaspoon gypsum with grains at mash
1	teaspoon gypsum with sparge
	Wyeast No. 1098 liquid yeast

Original specific gravity: 1.051
Final specific gravity: 1.016
Boiling time: 60 minutes
Primary fermentation: six days at 65 degrees F (18.5 degrees C) in glass
Secondary fermentation: 18 days at 50 degrees F (10 degrees C) in stainless steel
Age when judged (since bottling): one month

Brewer's specifics

Mash grains for 30 minutes at 129 degrees F (54 degrees C). Raise temperature to 152.5 degrees F (67 degrees C) and hold for 90 minutes. Sparge with 3 1/2 gallons of 158-degree-F (67-degree-C) water.

Judges' comments

"Spicy hop aroma. Sweet, slightly fruity start. Clean, soft finish. A nice clean beer. Body and mouthfeel are great."

"Hints of hop, fruitiness and some graininess. Clean, malty, dry, good balance, nicely soft on palate. Hop flavor a bit big for style. Nice finish. Original gravity may be a tad high for category. Nice drinking brew — great job. Just a little 'big' in some ways for style. I suggest cutting back original gravity and flavoring hops a bit."

LEAGUE CITY ALT PART 3

Düsseldorf-style Altbier
First Place, German-style Ale, 1991
Steven and Christina Daniel, League City, Texas
(all grain)

Ingredients for 5 gallons

8	pounds two-row malt
2	pounds crystal malt
2	pounds Munich malt,
3/4	ounce (26 IBU) Perle hops (90 minutes)
	Wyeast No. 2308 liquid lager yeast

Original specific gravity: 1.054
Final specific gravity: 1.017
Boiling time: 90 minutes
Primary fermentation: three weeks at 50 degrees F (10 degrees C) in stainless steel
Secondary fermentation: four weeks at 32 degrees F (0 degrees C) in stainless steel
Age when judged (since bottling): one month

Brewers' specifics

Mash grains one hour at 152 degrees F (66.5 degrees C).
Force carbonate in keg, counterpressure bottle.

Judges' comments

"Very nice color, clarity, and head. Firm malt palate, smooth and well-balanced. Some more hop flavor would be nice. Nice rendition of style. Not much to fault. A tad more hop flavor and maltiness is all this beer needs."

"Nice malt aroma, maybe a hint of fruitiness. A bit of toasted malt flavor. Nice malt character but needs more bitterness in finish. Nice beer. Could use more boiling hops for character in finish."

XMAS EVE KÖLSCH

Kölsch
Second Place, German-style Ale, 1993
Bruce Cornell, Baton Rouge, Louisiana
(grain/extract)

Ingredients for 5 gallons

4	pounds Alexander's pale malt extract
2	pounds American Eagle light dry malt extract
1	pound Munich malt
1/4	pound crystal malt
3/4	ounce Perle hops, 6.8 percent alpha acid (60 minutes)
1/2	ounce Perle hops, 6.8 percent alpha acid (30 minutes)
1/2	ounce Tettnanger hops, 4.2 percent alpha acid (two minutes)
	Wyeast No. 1007 liquid yeast culture
3/4	cup corn sugar for priming

Original specific gravity: 1.048
Final specific gravity: 1.024
Boiling time: 65 minutes
Primary fermentation: four days at 72 degrees F (22 degrees C) in plastic
Secondary fermentation: 13 days at 72 degrees F (22 degrees C) in glass
Age when judged (since bottling): six months

Brewer's specifics

Steep grains at 160 degrees F (71 degrees C) for 30 minutes.

Judges' comments

"Dry, bitter finish, medium bitterness. Deep golden color too dark for style. Hoppy aroma is too much for style. Very good."
"Very little hop or malt flavor. Slight sour aftertaste. Could use more hops."
"A little sweet, but dry finish. Pleasantly complex flavor that is hard to pin down. Very drinkable with a catchy flavor."
"Green, seaweedy. Lingering graininess. Good bitterness level and dryness."
"Malt okay. Good conditioning and balance."

CHAPTER 17

FRUIT BEER

The sky's the limit with fruit beers. Add fruit to any standard beer and you can come up with some startling and delicious flavors. In many cases, lighter beer styles are used, because darker, roastier beers can mask the taste of the fruit. If you want to experiment with fruit stouts, bocks, or other dark beers, be sure to use plenty of fruit to balance the malt flavors. The fruit you use should be pitted and crushed. Some brewers prefer to pasteurize the fruit they are using. It's a wide open style, so go ahead and experiment.

AHA National Homebrew Competition Style Guidelines
a) Fruit Beer – Any ale or lager made with fruit. Character of fruit should be evident in color, aroma, and flavor. Body, color, hop character, and strength can vary greatly.
b) Classic-style Fruit Beer – Any classic style of ale or lager to which fruit has been added. Brewer to specify style.

OG (Balling/Plato)	Percent alc./vol.	IBUs	SRM
a) Fruit Beer			
1.030-1.110 (7.5-27.5)	2.5-12%	5-70	5-50
b) Classic-style Fruit Beer			
(refer to individual styles)			

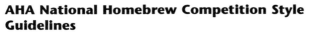

LEFTOVER STRAWBERRY ALE

Fruit Beer
First Place, Fruit Beer, 1992
Dan Robison, Salt Lake City, Utah
(all grain)

Ingredients for 4 1/2 gallons

7	pounds two-row Klages malt
1	pound dextrin malt
1/2	ounce Chinook hops (90 minutes)
1	ounce Cascade hops (finish)
	Wyeast No. 1056 liquid yeast
9	pounds frozen strawberries

Original specific gravity: 1.050
Final specific gravity: 1.011
Boiling time: 90 minutes
Primary fermentation: seven days at 65 degrees F (18 degrees C) in stainless steel
Secondary fermentation: seven days at 65 degrees F (18 degrees C) in stainless steel
Age when judged (since bottling): seven months

Brewer's specifics

Mash grains at 158 degrees F (70 degrees C) for 90 minutes.
Add frozen strawberries to primary fermenter.

Judges' comments

"Thirst quenching. May want just a little more malt or a yeast that is not so attenuative to provide a little sweetness for balance. Very impressive."
"Nice effort. Strawberry evident!"
"Tartness of fruit is evident and nicely balanced by beer maltiness. Very nice."
"Good tasting fruit beer. Good job. Well done."

3-DIMENSIONAL RASPBERRY ALE

Fruit Beer
First Place, Fruit Beer, 1990
John Abbott, Chico, California
(extract)

Ingredients for 5 gallons

5	pounds Alexander's light malt extract
1/6	ounce Saaz hop pellets (60 minutes)
1/6	ounce Saaz hop pellets (45 minutes)
1/6	ounce Saaz hop pellets (two minutes)
6	pounds frozen red raspberries
1 2/3	ounces M.eV. No. 004 liquid ale yeast
3/4	cup dextrose to prime

Original specific gravity: 1.033
Final specific gravity: 1.006
Primary fermentation: four days at 70 degrees F (21 degrees C) in glass
Secondary fermentation: three weeks at 70 degrees F (21 degrees C) in glass
Age when judged (since bottling): 6 1/2 months

Judges' comments

"Very raspberry! Nice color; clear but not brilliant. Flavor is a bit sour, but nice! Like a lambic framboise. Could use a little more hops. Great body! Wow! Like Lindemann's Framboise. I want more."

"Slightly sour, creamy aroma. A kiss of hops comes through. Beautiful color and clarity. Nice lactic, malty flavor coupled with raspberry and slight hops. Creamy like triple cream brie — lovely. Overall a beautiful beer. Apéritif or summer cooler."

"Nice bouquet. Slight sour tone in aroma. Excellent bubbles. Good clarity and color. Nice creamy mouthfeel. Definite sour profile; sourness tends to dominate a tad too much. Nice beer. Maybe sour tone could be cut back ever so slightly."

BLACK RASPBERRY ALE

Fruit Beer
First Place, Fruit Beer, 1991
Ken Kraemer, Bloomington, Minnesota
(extract/grain)

Ingredients for 5 gallons

5	pounds Munton and Fison light dry malt extract
11	ounces Munton and Fison diastatic malt extract
12	ounces two-row malt
8	ounces wheat malt
8	ounces 90 °L crystal malt
8	ounces chocolate malt
6	ounces black patent malt
1	ounce Cluster hops, 9 percent alpha acid (55 minutes)
1	ounce Cascade hops, 5.5 percent alpha acid (five minutes)
6	pounds black raspberries (steeped 30 minutes after boil)
	Wyeast No. 1028 London ale liquid yeast
3/4	cup corn sugar to prime

Original specific gravity: 1.051
Final specific gravity: 1.013
Boiling time: 60 minutes
Primary fermentation: 12 days at 65 degrees F (18.5 degrees C) in plastic
Secondary fermentation: nine days at 65 degrees F (18.5 degrees C) in glass
Age when judged (since bottling): five months

Brewer's specifics

Mash grains one hour at 152 degrees F (66.5 degrees F). Thaw frozen black raspberries before adding to wort at the end of the boil. Steep for 30 minutes. Chill wort and strain berries out as the wort is poured into the fermenter.

Judges' comments

"Nice delicate berry notes to nose. Clean as a whistle. Subtle aroma, nicely done. Richly complex — berry sweetness and tartness mingle nicely. A little more body would help. Very well-done beer. Rich berry sweetness nicely offset by tartness and hops."

"Nice raspberry aroma. A slight astringency but not offensive. Nice berry, malt, and hop balance lingering into aftertaste. A definitely drinkable brew, nicely balanced."

CHERRY ALE

Fruit Beer
First Place, Fruit Beer, 1989
David G. Hammaker, Roaring Spring, Pennsylvania
(extract)

Ingredients for 5 gallons

6	*pounds English light malt extract*
1/2	*ounce Bullion hop pellets (45 minutes)*
1	*ounce Hallertauer hop pellets (10 minutes)*
10	*pounds sweet cherries*
2	*packets Red Star ale yeast*
3/4	*cup corn sugar to prime*

Original specific gravity: not given
Final specific gravity: not given
Boiling time: 60 minutes
Primary fermentation: two weeks at 60 degrees F (15.5 degrees
C) in glass
Secondary fermentation: 10 weeks at 60 degrees F (15.5
degrees C) in glass
Age when judged (since bottling): four years

Brewer's specifics

After boil, pour wort over cherries. Cool and add yeast. After
two weeks, transfer to secondary.

Judges' comments

*"Fabulous cherry and malt aroma. Quite clear. Bold cherry compo-
nent needs time to blend with malt. Some diacetyl character but
appropriate for style. Mouth-coating. Could use a bit more hops."*
*"A good blend of hops, malt, and cherries; one aroma doesn't over-
power the others. Clear with good head retention. A slight hop flavor
along with the cherry tartness. Slightly acidic."*
*"Strong and clean aroma. Very bright appearance. Wonderful bal-
ance and flavor. A dandy overall."*

CHAPTER 18

HERB BEER

Before brewers added hops to beer, all different kinds of herbs and spices were added to balance the malt sweetness. This style is another wide open category where you can experiment at will. Nutmeg, cinnamon, cloves, and ginger are among the most popular spices used by modern brewers, although peppers, anise, coriander, and orange peel are also employed. Keep in mind that many herbs and spices are very potent. Only a small amount is needed in most cases to get a super spicy character.

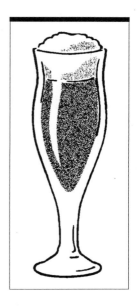

AHA National Homebrew Competition Style Guidelines
a) **Herb Beer** – Any ale or lager with herbs. Character of herb or spice should be evident in aroma and flavor. Body, color, hop character, and strength can vary greatly.
b) **Classic-style Herb Beer** – Any classic style of ale or lager to which herbs have been added. Brewer to specify style.

OG (Balling/Plato)	Percent alc./vol.	IBUs	SRM
a) Herb Beer			
1.030-1.110 (7.5-27.5)	2.5-12%	5-70	5-50
b) Classic-style Herb Beer			
(refer to individual styles)			

HERB ALPERT

Herb Lager
Second Place, Herb Beer, 1991
Ron Page, Middletown, Connecticut
(all grain)

Ingredients for 11 gallons

30	pounds Pilsener malt
1	pound Munich malt
1	ounce chocolate malt
1	ounce Saaz hops
1 1/3	ounces Tettnanger hops
1 1/2	ounces Mount Hood hops
11	chamomile tea bags (added to fermenter)
60	dried marigold blossoms (added to fermenter)
	Wyeast No. 2206 liquid yeast

Original specific gravity: 1.060
Final specific gravity: 1.016
Primary fermentation: one week at 50 degrees F (10 degrees C) in stainless steel
Secondary fermentation: three weeks at 40 degrees F (4.5 degrees C) in stainless steel
Age when judged (since bottling): not given

Judges' comments

"Hoppy/herbaceous aroma, no off-aromas. Crystal clear, great head retention. Lingering herb flavor, excellent balance. This is an extremely well-made beer. Unfortunately, I'm not sure I can fully appreciate it since I'm not familiar with marigold and chamomile!"

"Fragrant floral aroma. Hoppy, slight sweetness. Floral, orange flavor with sweet, fragrant chamomile. Nice, slighty minty. A well-made beer. Good amount of herb, though not exactly my cup of beer."

FRIENDLY SPRUCE LAGER

NOTES

Herb Lager
First Place, Herb Beer, 1989
Mark C. Fjeld, West Valley City, Utah
(extract)

Ingredients for 5 gallons

4	pounds Mountmellick light lager hopped malt extract
4	pounds clover honey
1/2	ounce Tettnanger hops (10 minutes)
1	pint jar new spruce growth (10 minutes)
2	packets Mountmellick lager yeast
3/4	cup corn sugar to prime

Original specific gravity: 1.036
Final specific gravity: 1.004
Boiling time: 60 minutes
Primary fermentation: three weeks at 74 degrees F (23.3 degrees C) in glass
Age when judged (since bottling): 12 months

Brewer's specifics

Honey added at beginning of boil. Spruce growth added with hops.

Judges' comments

"Nice fresh aroma. Spruce is apparent; very pleasant. Pretty beer; greenish tinge. Nice and clear. Good head beading. Nice flavor from spruce; resiny. Sweet but not cloying, smooth. It's like Christmas trees! Very good beer."

"Spruce and honey aroma. Very clear — excellent clarity. Frothy, creamy head with good beading. Nice tang of spruce. It does taste like spruce. Well-balanced beer. Very pleasing and refreshing beer!"

"Surprising, like a walk in the woods. Sweet up front, dry finish. Very good, refreshing, crisp."

CHILE GARDEN PILS

Herb Beer
First Place, Herb Beer, 1992
Eric McClary, Carson City, Nevada
(all grain)

Ingredients for 5 gallons

9	pounds Klages malt
1	pound toasted Klages malt
2	ounces Saaz hops (60 minutes)
1 1/4	ounces Saaz hops (10 minutes)
3/4	ounce Saaz hops (steeped 15 minutes after boil)
6	deseeded Fresno chilies (steeped 15 minutes after boil)
	Wyeast No. 2206 liquid yeast
3/4	cup dextrose to prime

Original specific gravity: 1.051
Final specific gravity: 1.008
Boiling time: 60 minutes
Primary fermentation: seven days at 55 degrees F (13 degrees C) in glass
Secondary fermentation: 50 days at 38 degrees F (3 degrees C) in glass
Age when judged (since bottling): seven months

Brewer's specifics

Toast one pound Klages for 10 minutes at 300 degrees F (150 degrees C). Mash grains at 128 degrees F (54 degrees C) for 45 minutes. Raise temperature to 154 degrees F (68 degrees C) for 90 minutes. Steep chilies and aroma hops at end of boil.

Judges' comments

"Good chili flavor without burning your mouth out. Very creamy. Good balance. Pleasantly subtle."
"The peppers are added in just the right amount, they augment the flavor, but don't overpower it."
"Fascinating. Not what I expected. Pepper flavor definitely there."
"Surprisingly tasty and easy to drink. Fresh chili-pepper flavor shines through. This could grow on you."

LOOSE LUCY GINGER LAGER

Herb Beer
First Place, Herb Beer, 1991
Gene Muller, Westmont, New Jersey
(extract)

Ingredients for 5 gallons

4 1/2   pounds Laaglander light malt extract
1 1/2   pounds honey
3   ounces freshly grated ginger root
1   ounce Cascade hops (60 minutes)
1/2   ounce Cascade hops (30 minutes)
          Zest of four oranges (10 minutes)
1/2   ounce Cascade hops (two minutes)
          M.eV. American lager liquid yeast
3/4   cup corn sugar to prime

Original specific gravity: not given
Final specific gravity: not given
Boiling time: 60 minutes
Primary fermentation: six days at 50 degrees F (10 degrees C) in glass
Secondary fermentation: 13 days at 50 degrees F (10 degrees C) in glass
Age when judged (since bottling): two months

Brewer's specifics

Spices added at beginning of boil, orange zest for last 10 minutes of boil.

Judges' comments

"Beautiful ginger, honey aroma with citrus overtones. Nice flavor, doesn't bang you over the head. I love the beer."
"Floral, orangey, sweet, slight tartness in aroma. Honey, slight bitterness, and ginger in flavor. Delicate and refreshing. Nice delicate light lager, good job of matching spice level to body and flavor of beer. Well made!"

Wissahickon Holiday Spiced Ale

Herb Beer
Second Place, Herb Beer, 1989
David J. Perlman, Philadelphia, Pennsylvania
(extract)

Ingredients for 5 gallons

3 1/3	pounds John Bull amber malt extract
3 1/3	pounds Munton and Fison light malt extract
3/4	pound light dry malt extract
1	pound dry maltodextrin (65 minutes)
1 1/2	ounces Cascade hops (65 minutes)
1	ounce Bullion hops (65 minutes)
2	ounces grated ginger (25 minutes)
2	teaspoons cinnamon (25 minutes)
1	teaspoon ground coriander (25 minutes)
7	small cloves (25 minutes)
1	ounce Kent Goldings hop pellets (dry)
	Wyeast No. 1098 British Ale liquid yeast
3/4	cup corn sugar

Original specific gravity: 1.057
Final specific gravity: 1.025
Boiling time: 65 minutes
Primary fermentation: two weeks at 70 degrees F (21 degrees C) in glass
Age when judged (since bottling): two months

Brewer's specifics

Add ginger, cinnamon, coriander, and cloves for the last 25 minutes of the boil.

Judges' comments

"Fresh aroma — ginger predominates a little, but nice blend. Nice light amber color, clear, good head retention. Very nice flavor; well-blended. An excellent, well-made beer."

"Smells great; all spices are quite apparent. Sounds good too. Slightly cloudy but OK for an ale. Beautiful beading in head. Beer is creamy with good color. Refreshing, cloves really kick in. Maybe ease up on them a little to allow other spices to be perceived. Wonderful holiday beer!"

"Very pleasant, fresh aroma. Great head and color. Tastes great, but I expected more body. Overall a great job."

CHAPTER 19

SPECIALTY BEER

Maple syrup, chocolate, potatoes, and nuts have all been used in beer, each lending its own unique flavor to the finished brew. Beers that use unusual procedures are also in this genre. Steinbier is a traditional beer that uses white-hot rocks in the wort to produce a characteristic flavor. Your imagination is the only limitation here.

AHA National Homebrew Competition Style Guidelines

Any ale or lager brewed using unusual techniques and/or fermentable ingredients other than (or in addition to) malted barley as a unique contribution to the overall character of the beer. Examples include (but are not limited to) the use of honey and maple sap or syrup or heating the wort with white-hot stones. Examples do not include fruit or herbs, though they can be used to add to the character of other uniquely fermentable ingredients.

a) Specialty Beer – Any non-classic style fitting the above description.

b) Classic-style Specialty Beer – Any classic ale or lager to which special ingredients or special process has been used, for example, honey Pilsener, maple porter, sorghum stout, pumpkin pale ale. Brewer to specify style.

OG (Balling/Plato)	Percent alc./vol.	IBUs	SRM
a) Specialty Beer			
1.030-1.110 (7.5-27.5)	2.5-12%	0-100	0-100
b) Classic-style Specialty Beer			
(refer to individual styles)			

1991 CHRISTMAS ALE

Specialty Beer
First Place, Specialty Beer, 1992
Bob Barson, Chicago, Illinois
(grain/extract)

Ingredients for 5 gallons

6 2/3	pounds Northwestern Gold malt extract
2	pounds Munton and Fison dark dry malt extract
1 1/2	pounds Munich malt
1 1/2	pounds Vienna malt
1	pound 90 °L crystal malt
6	ounces dextrin powder
1/2	ounce Cascade hops, 4.9 percent alpha acid (90 minutes)
1/2	ounce Kent Goldings hops, 5.9 percent alpha acid (90 minutes)
1 1/2	pounds Sioux Bee Clover Honey (90 minutes)
3/4	pound Grandma's Robust Style Molasses (90 minutes)
1/2	ounce Willamette hops, 4.5 percent alpha acid (30 minutes)
1/2	ounce Willamette hops, 4.5 percent alpha acid (two minutes)
1 1/2	ounce Cascade hops, 4.9 percent alpha acid (dry)
1	ounce Kent Goldings hops, 5.5 percent alpha acid (dry)
8	whole cloves (dry)
750	mL Le Roux Triple Sec (aged 5 1/2 weeks with three whole cloves)
3	teaspoons pumpkin pie spice
4	teaspoons dried orange zest
1	ounce pure almond extract
	Whitbread Ale yeast
8	teaspoons calcium sulfate
1	teaspoon salt
1	teaspoon Irish moss

Original specific gravity: 1.090
Final specific gravity: 1.020
Boiling time: 90 minutes
Primary fermentation: five days at 60 degrees F (15 degrees C) in plastic
Secondary fermentation: 35 days at 60 degrees F (15 degrees C) in glass
Age when judged (since bottling): seven months

Brewer's specifics

Mash grains for 45 minutes at 150 degrees F (65 degrees C). Primed with LeRoux Triple Sec liqueur, pumpkin pie spice, dried orange zest, and pure almond extract.

Judges' comments

"Very nice effort. I'd like one of these at a Christmas party. A bit dry in body but still excellent."
"Wow! The whole kitchen is here. Good!"
"I couldn't drink more than one of these at a sitting, but I still like it. Ambitious beer. Well-brewed."

STEAMIN' HONEY WHEAT LAGER

Specialty Beer
Second Place, Specialty Beer, 1991
Scott Graysmith, Denver, Colorado
(grain/extract)

Ingredients for 5 gallons

4	pounds English lager malt
2	pounds wheat malt
3 1/3	pounds Munton and Fison wheat malt extract
1 1/2	ounces Hallertauer hops, 4.25 percent alpha acid (75 minutes)
1/2	ounce Saaz hops, 3.03 percent alpha acid (40 minutes)
1 1/2	pounds honey (30 minutes)
1/2	ounce Saaz hops, 3.03 percent alpha acid (20 minutes)
1/2	ounce Hallertauer hops, 4.25 percent alpha acid (five minutes)
1/2	ounce Saaz hops, 3.03 percent alpha acid (five minutes)
2	whole cloves (dry)
2	packages No. 2007 liquid lager yeast
2	packages Bavarian wheat beer yeast at bottling
1/2	cup honey to prime

Original specific gravity: 1.052
Final specific gravity: 1.010
Boiling time: 75 minutes
Primary fermentation: seven days at 65 degrees F (18 degrees C) in glass
Secondary fermentation: 17 days at 65 degrees F (18 degrees C) in glass
Age when judged (since bottling): two months

Brewer's specifics

Mash grains at 104 degrees F (40 degrees C) for 50 minutes, 122 degrees F (50 degrees C) for 45 minutes, 143 degrees F (62 degrees C) for 45 minutes, 155 degrees F (68 degrees C) for 35 minutes, and 170 degrees F (76 degrees C) to end mash.

Judges' comments

"Well-made beer. Clean and malty. Clove subtle and honey nonexistent. Otherwise a great beer."
"Nice drinkable beer. Nice balance. Cloves finish nicely. Could use a touch more honey. I like this combination of honey and cloves."
"Cloves don't come through as I would have expected from the nose. Slightly tart finish. Clean beer, but I wish the cloves had come through."
"Honey character comes through in flavor. Condition is OK but quickly falls flat by swallow. Clove taste not discernible. Lovely beer, nicely balanced."

ANNE'S CHOICE CHRISTMAS ALE

Specialty Beer
First Place, Specialty Beer, 1990
Philip Fleming, Broomfield, Colorado
(extract)

Ingredients for 5 gallons

3 1/2	pounds Munton and Fison malt extract stout kit
3 1/3	pounds Munton and Fison amber malt extract
3	pounds Munton and Fison amber dry malt extract
1/2	ounce Hallertauer hops (55 minutes)
3/4	pound honey (simmer 45 minutes)
5	three-inch cinnamon sticks (simmer 45 minutes)
2	teaspoons allspice (simmer 45 minutes)
1	teaspoon cloves (simmer 45 minutes)
6	ounces ginger root (simmer 45 minutes)
6	rinds from medium-sized oranges (simmer 45 minutes)
1/2	ounce Hallertauer hops (five minutes)
	Wyeast No. 1007 German ale liquid yeast
7	ounces corn sugar for priming

Original specific gravity: 1.069
Final specific gravity: 1.030
Primary fermentation: 14 days at 61 degrees F (16 degrees C) in glass
Age when judged (since bottling): six months

Brewer's specifics

Simmer spices and honey for 45 minutes. Boil malt and hops 50 minutes. Add finishing hops and boil five minutes. Cool, strain, and pitch yeast.

Judges' comments

"Cloves dominate aroma. Nice creamy head. Wonderful Christmas spices. This is what I call a spice beer. Full-bodied and very spicy with a sweet finish which is difficult to accomplish with all the spices. Great effort."

"Inviting aroma, lots of spice. Good appearance although hazy. All the specialty ingredients are present. Good warming, lingering taste. It could be sweeter; too bland in finish. OK body, but could be fuller. Overall an enjoyable holiday beer. Well made."

"Plenty of spice in nose. I can detect some clove. Good head retention. Clarity OK. Color is not sharp or brilliant. Flavor has cloves all over with a warming cinnamon backing. Body is OK, except that it thins out in the end. Nice winter warmer spice beer. Plenty of spice abounds."

GOTTLIEB'S VICTORY BEER NO. 11

Specialty Beer
First Place, Specialty Beer, 1989
Victor Gottlieb, Manakin-Sabot, Virginia
(grain/extract)

Ingredients for 5 gallons

3 1/3	pounds Munton and Fison light malt extract
3	pounds L.D. Carlson amber dry malt extract
1 1/2	cups crystal malt
4 1/4	pounds orange blossom honey
2	ounces Willamette hops (50 minutes)
1	ounce Cascade hops (50 minutes)
1/2	ounce Willamette hops (five minutes)
1/3	ounce Hallertauer hop pellets (five minutes)
1/3	ounce Saaz hop pellets (five minutes)
6	home-grown Chinook hops (five minutes)
1	packet Edme ale yeast
3/4	cup corn sugar

Original specific gravity: not given
Final specific gravity: not given
Boiling time: 50 minutes
Primary fermentation: four weeks at 60 degrees F (15.5 degrees C) in glass
Secondary fermentation: two weeks at 60 degrees F (15.5 degrees C) in glass
Age when judged (since bottling): four months

Brewer's specifics

Heat crystal malt to boiling in 16 ounces water. Strain malt and add liquid to 1 1/2 gallons water. Add malt extract and boiling hops, boil.
Turn off heat and add honey immediately. After 10 minutes, add one-half ounce Willamette hops. Steep three minutes and add one-third ounce Hallertauer pellets. Steep two minutes and sparge.
Dry hop on eighth day. Rack to secondary at two weeks, bottle at four weeks.

Judges' comments

"Alcoholic, malty aroma; initial hop aroma is clean. Appearance couldn't get much better. This beer has wonderful color, is clear, and has a nice head. Very smooth flavor. The initial sweetness is well-balanced with hop dryness. Overall a very drinkable, well-made beer."
"Beautiful floral, hoppy aroma with a slight hint of malt underneath and a tang of honey. It's a beauty — what more can I say? It is quite malty. Expected a little more hop bitterness. A well-balanced beer. Send me a case! And the recipe!"
"Alcoholic aroma, aromatic. Very good color, beading and head retention. Malty flavor with dryness bordering on caramelized. Good balance."

OLD MAPLE DOG

Classic-style Specialty Beer (Maple Barley Wine)
Second Place, Specialty Beer, 1992
Rob Lillard, Lyons, Colorado
(grain/extract)

Ingredients for 5 gallons

8	pounds Yellow Dog malt extract
3	pounds Munton and Fison amber dry malt extract
1	pound Munich malt
1/2	pound crystal malt
1/2	pound wheat malt
1	quart pure dark amber Grade A maple syrup
2	ounces Eroica hops (60 minutes)
1	ounce Eroica hops (30 minutes)
1	ounce Fuggles hops (steeped 15 minutes after boil)
1	ounce Fuggles hops (dry)
1	ounce Willamette hops (dry)
	Whitbread yeast
5/8	cup corn sugar to prime

Original specific gravity: 1.104
Final specific gravity: 1.038
Boiling time: 60 minutes
Primary fermentation: six days at 65 degrees F (18 degrees C) in glass
Secondary fermentation: 16 days at 65 degrees F (18 degrees C) in glass
Age when judged (since bottling): seven months

Brewer's specifics

Mash grains at 155 degrees F (68 degrees C) for 60 minutes.
Add maple syrup after the boil.

Judges' comments

"Nice smooth flavor. No off-flavors. Maple comes through. Very nice barley wine. Maple makes it that much better. Better than some commercial brews I have tried."
"Malty, alcoholic. Maple barely comes through. Well-brewed beer."

CHOCOLATE CHAMBORD STOUT

Classic-style Specialty Beer
First Place, Specialty Beer, 1993
Ron Page, Middletown, Connecticut
(all grain)

Ingredients for 4 1/2 gallons

7 1/2	pounds pale malt
1 1/2	pounds wheat malt
1/2	pound crystal malt
1/2	pound chocolate malt
1/2	pound flaked barley
4	AAUs Cascade hops (60 minutes)
4	AAUs Perle hops (60 minutes)
1/4	pound Hershey's cocoa powder (30 minutes)
1	tablespoon Chambord liqueur per bottle at capping

Original specific gravity: 1.052
Final specific gravity: not given
Boiling time: 60 minutes
Primary fermentation: three weeks at 65 degrees F (18 degrees C) in stainless steel
Secondary fermentation: six weeks at 35 degrees F (2 degrees C) in stainless steel
Age when judged (since bottling): not given

Brewer's specifics

Mash grains at 152 degrees F (67 degrees C) for one hour. Use chocolate in boil for 30 minutes.
Force carbonated.

Judges' comments

"Nice raspberry, nice chocolate, but where is the stout? No clear roast barley flavor. Finish too sweet for stout. Needs more balance."
"Nice balance. Long lasting aftertaste."
"Nice chocolate-raspberry flavor with bitter aftertaste of hops and raspberry. Nice balance!"
"Delicious raspberry/vanilla flavor. Slight charcoal flavor. Should have more hop bitterness for a dry stout."

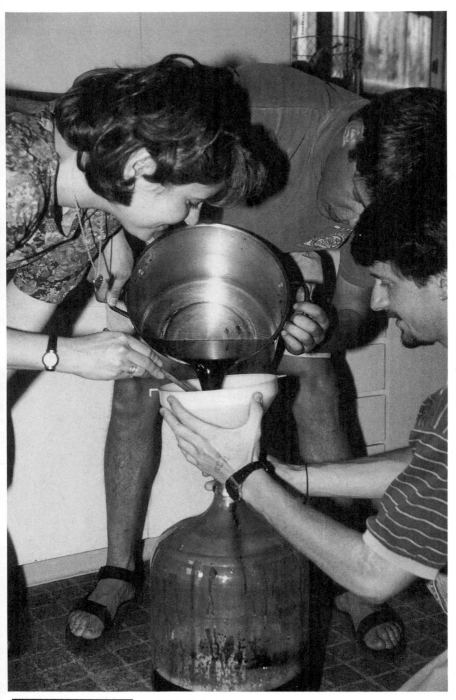

CHAPTER 20

SMOKED BEER

Using malt kilned over burning wood, smoked beer is a highly unusual taste experience. A good smoked beer has smoke in the aroma and flavor. The smoke flavor can come from "liquid" smoke, although some brewers do not believe this delivers a genuine smoky flavor and aroma. You can smoke your own grain in a smoker or on a barbecue grill using a fine mesh screen. Use a fragrant wood (beechwood is popular), and experiment a bit with the smoked malt in your recipe so you achieve the desired smoky aroma and flavor. Lovers of smoked beer believe that smoked cheeses and sausages are perfect partners for this unusual but taste-worthy beer.

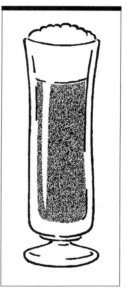

AHA National Homebrew Competition Style Guidelines
a) Bamberg-style Rauchbier – Oktoberfest style (see Oktoberfest) with a sweet smoky aroma and flavor. Dark amber to dark brown. Intensity of smoke medium to high. Low diacetyl OK.
b) Other (brewer to specify style) – All other beer styles as so designated by brewer with smoke flavor.

OG (Balling/Plato)	Percent alc./vol.	IBUs	SRM
a) Bamberg-style Rauchbier			
1.048-52 (12-13)	4.3-4.8%	20-30	10-20
b) Other			
(refer to individual styles)			

PRAIRIE SMOKED BEER

Bamberg-style Rauchbier
Second Place, Smoked Beer, 1991
Dave Lipitz, Judy Lipitz, and Lynn Patterson, Pueblo, Colorado
(all grain)

Ingredients for 5 gallons

4	pounds pale malt
2	pounds lager malt
2 1/2	pounds Munich malt
1/2	pound crystal malt
1/4	pound dextrin malt
1/4	pound red roasted barley
3/4	ounce home-grown Hallertauer hops (60 minutes)
1/4	ounce Northern Brewer hops, 9.4 percent alpha acid (60 minutes)
1/2	ounce Mount Hood hops, 3.5 percent alpha acid (30 minutes)
1/2	ounce Mount Hood hops, 3.5 percent alpha acid (10 minutes)
	Bavarian yeast No. 2206
2	teaspoons gypsum
3/4	cup corn sugar to prime

Original specific gravity: 1.055
Final specific gravity: 1.015
Boiling time: 60 minutes
Primary fermentation: seven days at 60 degrees F (15 degrees C) in glass
Secondary fermentation: 14 days at 60 degrees F (15 degrees C) in glass
Tertiary fermentation: one month at 32 degrees F (0 degrees C) in glass
Age when judged (since bottling): six months

Brewers' specifics

Soak Munich malt in water for 15 minutes then smoke over apple and beechwood. Mash grains at 145 degrees F (63 degrees C) for 20 minutes. Raise temperature to 159 degrees F (71 degrees C) until conversion. Sparge with 4 gallons of 170-degree-F (77-degree-C) water.

Judges' comments

"Medium smoky flavor. Slight maltiness. Slight astringency."
"Nice smoky notes. Slight astringency noticeable in aftertaste. Very good effort."

BEECH BEER

Bamberg-style Rauchbier
First Place, Smoked Beer, 1992
James Cannon, Williamsburg, Virginia
(all grain)

Ingredients for 5 gallons

2 1/2	pounds smoked Klages malt
2 1/4	pounds Munich malt
1	pound Vienna malt
4 1/2	pounds Klages malt
1/2	pound 40 °L crystal malt
1	ounce Hallertauer hops (105 minutes)
1/2	ounce Hallertauer hops (15 minutes)
1/4	ounce Hallertauer hops (two minutes)
1/4	ounce Saaz hops (dry)
	Wyeast No. 2206 liquid yeast
2/3	cup dextrose to prime

Original specific gravity: 1.054
Final specific gravity: 1.013
Boiling time: 105 minutes
Primary fermentation: 28 days at 50 degrees F (10 degrees C) in glass
Secondary fermentation: 28 days at 35 degrees F (2 degrees C) in glass
Age when judged (since bottling): three months

Brewer's specifics

Smoke 2 1/2 pounds Klages malt on a grill over smoldering local beechwood for 30 minutes. Mash grains at 105 degrees F (41 degrees C) for 20 minutes. First decoction to 125 degrees F (52 degrees C) for 10 minutes. Second decoction to 149 degrees F (65 degrees C). Cool to 144 degrees F (62 degrees C) over 30-minute period. Raise temperature to 154 degrees F (68 degrees C) for 30 minutes. Raise again to 168 degrees F (75 degrees C). Sparge with 6 gallons of 168-degree-F (75-degree-C) water.

Judges' comments

"Very good, delicate smoke but good balance."
"Good malt and smoke synergy. Some DMS problems. Some vegetable overtones."
"Very nice smoke flavor. Decent body. Good clean, smoke finish. Maybe just a little thin."
"Very good, but has some warm ferment characters. Otherwise a well wrought, beautifully smoked beer."

SMOKEHOUSE LAGER

Bamberg-style Rauchbier
Second Place, Smoked Beer, 1989
John Maier, Juneau, Alaska
(all grain)

Ingredients for 5 gallons

8 1/2	pounds Klages pale two-row malt
1 1/2	pounds 10 °L Munich malt smoked over alderwood
1 1/2	pounds 120 °L caramel malt
2/3	pound 40 °L caramel malt
2/3	pound CaraPils malt
3/4	ounce Perle hop pellets (75 minutes)
3/4	ounce Perle hop pellets (60 minutes)
3/4	ounce U.S. Hallertauer Mittelfrueh hop pellets (finish)
1/50	ounce gypsum per gallon of mash and sparge water
48	ounces Yeastbank ybL2 lager yeast starter
1/16	teaspoon Yeastex yeast nutrient
5	ounces dextrose to prime

Original specific gravity: 1.047
Final specific gravity: 1.014
Boiling time: 90 minutes
Primary fermentation: 1 1/2 weeks at 55 degrees F (13 degrees C) in glass
Secondary fermentation: five days at 55 degrees F (13 degrees C) in glass
Age when judged (since bottling): two months

Brewer's specifics

Mash grains at 120 degrees F (49 degrees C) for 30 minutes, raise temperature to 130 degrees F (54.5 degrees C). Infuse boiling water to raise temperature to 150 degrees F (65.5 degrees C). Hold for 30 minutes; raise temperature to 170 degrees F (76.5 degrees C). Transfer to lauter-tun, sparge with 170-degree-F (76.5-degree-C) water to collect 8 1/4 gallons of wort.

Judges' comments

"Great aroma, malt comes through, smoke is not overpowering. Good color for category. Very clear, nice creamy head. Slight astringency. Very drinkable. Astringency may be from overboiling of grains."
"Good malt aroma; hop aroma is light. Very clear, dark, nut-brown color. Slightly astringent. Has a strong aftertaste that lingers. A good beer."
"Smoke aroma very slight. Very good appearance. Flavor is very nice. Overall a nice beer."

SMOKY MASH

Bamberg-style Rauchbier
Third Place, Smoked Beer, 1989
Ralph Bucca, Huntingtown, Maryland
(all grain)

Ingredients for 1 gallon
(You'll brew five gallons and use one gallon to make Smokey Mash.)

10	*pounds pale malt*
2/3	*ounce Cluster hops (60 minutes)*
1 1/4	*tablespoon liquid smoke (boiled)*
1	*packet Edme ale yeast*
1	*ounce sugar to prime*

Original specific gravity: 1.035
Final specific gravity: 1.000
Boiling time: 60 minutes
Primary fermentation: three weeks at 65 degrees F (18.5 degrees C) in glass
Secondary fermentation: two weeks at 65 degrees F (18.5 degrees C) in glass
Age when judged (since bottling): three months

Brewer's specifics
Mash with 3 gallons for one hour at 155 degrees F (68.5 degrees C). Sparge with 3 gallons water. Draw 1 gallon from 5-gallon mash, boil with the Clusters and liquid smoke.

Judges' comments
"Somewhat light aroma. Appearance is nice and clean. Overall a good beer."
"Smoke aroma is weak. Appearance is nice and clear; good carbonation. Aftertaste jumps out at you. Overall pretty good."

KILTS ON FIRE

Smoked Scottish Wee Heavy
First Place, Smoked Beer, 1993
Paddy Giffen, Cotati, California
1993 Homebrewer of the Year
(all grain)

Ingredients for 5 gallons

4	pounds smoked Pilsener malt
4 1/2	pounds Belgium Pilsener malt
5	pounds amber dry malt extract
1	pound CaraVienne malt
3/4	pound Special "B" malt
1	pound Munich malt
1	pound British crystal malt
1/4	ounce Chinook hops (60 minutes)
1/4	ounce Chinook hops (30 minutes)
1/4	ounce British Blend hops (30 minutes)
1/2	ounce Liberty hops (30 minutes)
	Wyeast No. 1084 liquid yeast culture

Original specific gravity: 1.088
Final specific gravity: 1.038
Boiling time: 60 minutes
Primary fermentation: 11 days at 65 degrees F (18 degrees C) in glass
Secondary fermentation: eight weeks at 65 degrees F (18 degrees C) in glass
Age when judged (since bottling): four months

Brewer's specifics

Mash grains for 85 minutes at 154 degrees F (68 degrees C).
Force carbonate.

Judges' comments

"Strong malt and smoke tastes. They blend well together. Very drinkable smoked Scottish wee heavy, but you do have to sip it!"
"Very malty, nice smoke. Heavy! Puts hair on a chest. Nice job. I could only drink a half pint of this."
"Great malty flavor backed with fine smoke intensity. Superb in every respect. What a taste experience. On to the Best-of-Show."
"Excellent Scottish heavy. Sweet with good smoke character. Alcohol evident, but balanced."

CHAPTER 21

CALIFORNIA COMMON BEER

California Common Beer is a true, American-style beer. While origins of the style are unclear, the beer is generally lager-style, but with more estery and fruity qualities than traditional lagers. The warmer fermentation temperatures produce the yeast flavors needed, and the addition of some caramel malts will bring your beer closer to commercial examples. Northern Brewer hops are an excellent choice for this beer.

AHA National Homebrew Competition Style Guidelines

Light amber to copper. Medium body. Toasted or caramellike maltiness in aroma and flavor. Medium to high hop bitterness. Hop flavor medium to high. Aroma medium. Fruitiness and esters low. Low diacetyl OK. Lager yeast, fermented warm but aged cold.

OG (Balling/Plato)	Percent alc./vol.	IBUs	SRM
1.040-55 (10-14)	3.6-5%	35-45	8-17

MEMPHIS STEAMER

California Common Beer
First Place, California Common Beer, 1992
Phil Rahn, Cordova, Tennessee
(all grain)

Ingredients for 10 gallons

16 1/2	pounds Klages malt
2 1/2	pounds crystal malt
3 1/4	ounces Northern Brewer hops, 6.5 percent alpha acid (60 minutes)
3/4	ounce Cascade hops (60 minutes)
1 1/2	ounces Cascade hops (40 minutes)
1	ounce Centennial hops (finish)
1	ounce Cascade hops (dry)
	Wyeast No. 2206 liquid yeast

Original specific gravity: 1.049
Final specific gravity: 1.013
Boiling time: 60 minutes
Primary fermentation: 12 days at 68 degrees F (20 degrees C) in glass
Secondary fermentation: 10 days at 68 degrees F (20 degrees C) in glass
Age when judged (since bottling): eight months

Brewer's specifics

Mash grains at 155 degrees F (68 degrees C) for 90 minutes.

Judges' comments

"An excellent beer, but hop character overwhelms somewhat."
"Nice beer, just needs more hop bitterness for style."
"Good beer. Nice malt and hop flavor. Good balance. Nice hops."
"Lots of hops. Malt most apparent in finish. A touch of astringency. Tasty!"

SACRAMENTO STEAM BEER

California Common Beer
Second Place, California Common Beer, 1990
Ralph Housley, Sacramento, California
(extract)

Ingredients for 5 gallons

3	pounds Glenbrew malt extract
3	pounds Tom Caxton lager malt extract
1/4	ounce CFJ-90 hops (45 minutes)
1/4	ounce CFJ-90 hops (10 minutes)
1/4	ounce CFJ-4 hops (10 minutes)
1	ounce CFJ-90 hops (two minutes)
3/4	ounce CFJ-4 hops (dry hop — two weeks)
	Wyeast liquid lager yeast
	Corn sugar to prime

Original specific gravity: 1.046
Final specific gravity: 1.012
Primary fermentation: 16 days at 65 degrees F (18.5 degrees C) in glass
Secondary fermentation: six weeks at 65 degrees F (18.5 degrees C) in glass
Age when judged (since bottling): two months

Judges' comments

"Predominant hop nose, slight diacetyl. Color appropriate."
"Very drinkable. I would have a few of these. If you can make it richer it may be worth a try. Otherwise, good as is."
"Good malt hop balance, slightly sweet. Body appropriate for style. Slightly on the sweet side. Very good beer."
"Great appearance — perfect for style. Fruity, maybe needs cooler fermentation. Might do better as an ale. Slight bitter aftertaste. Very drinkable beer."
"Impressive head. Glorious color and clarity. Seemed a bit thin to me, but very close to style. Need to increase malt or decrease bittering hops slightly."

NUMBER 4

California Common Beer
Second Place, California Common Beer, 1991
Curtis Palm, Palouse, Washington
(grain/extract)

Ingredients for 5 gallons

7   *pounds amber malt extract*
3   *pounds two-row pale malt*
1   *pound toasted pale malt*
1/2   *pound dextrin malt*
3/4   *pound crystal malt*
2   *ounces Chinook hops (60 minutes)*
1   *ounce Cascade hops (60 minutes)*
1   *ounce Cascade hops (finish)*
         Wyeast Danish Lager liquid yeast slurry from starter
3/4   *cup fructose to prime*

Original specific gravity: 1.044
Final specific gravity: 1.011
Boiling time: 60 minutes
Primary fermentation: six days at 60 degrees F (15.5 degrees C) in plastic
Secondary fermentation: 19 days at 60 degrees F (15.5 degrees C) in glass
Age when judged (since bottling): 4 1/4 months

Brewer's specifics

Mash grains for 20 minutes at 120 degrees F (49 degrees C), then raise temperature to 155 degrees F (68.5 degrees C) for 30 minutes.

Judges' comments

"Smooth, high quality. Slightly salty finish is a bit odd. Conditioning is excellent."
"Too much hop bitterness for style."

FAT BROTHERS ORIGINAL AMERICAN

California Common Beer
First Place, California Common Beer, 1989
Stephen Morelli, Portland, Oregon
(grain/extract)

Ingredients for 5 gallons

7	pounds Steinbart's light malt extract
8	ounces 40 °L crystal malt
1	ounce Chinook hops (60 minutes)
1/2	ounce Cascade hops (60 minutes)
1	ounce Cascade hops (10 minutes)
	Wyeast lager liquid yeast
3/4	cup dextrose

Original specific gravity: 1.040
Final specific gravity: not given
Boiling time: 90 minutes
Primary fermentation: two weeks at 65 degrees F (18.5 degrees C) in glass
Secondary fermentation: one week at 65 degrees F (18.5 degrees C) in glass
Age when judged (since bottling): 6 1/2 months

Brewer's specifics

Steep crystal malt with 1 gallon water, bring to boiling then remove grains. Add 1 gallon preboiled water and malt extract.

Judges' comments

"Good hop aroma. No haze, good appearance. Full hop and malt flavor. Very good. No off-flavors."

"Nice malty nose. Head retention is very good. Nice malt and hop balance. A bit too alcoholic. Very drinkable."

"Nice hop aroma, with some malt. A bit murky. Some sourness, but the bitterness really has my tongue in a headlock."

AMBER

California Common Beer
Second Place, California Common Beer, 1989
Robert Carter, Watsonville, California
(all grain)

Ingredients for 5 gallons

8	pounds Klages malt
1	pound crystal malt
1	ounce Northern Brewer hops (60 minutes)
1	ounce Cascade hops (10 minutes)
1/4	ounce Cascade hops (dry)
	Brewer's Choice liquid lager yeast
3/4	cup corn sugar to prime

Original specific gravity: 1.050
Final specific gravity: 1.010
Boiling time: 60 minutes
Primary fermentation: one week at 60 degrees F (15.5 degrees C) in plastic
Secondary fermentation: two weeks at 60 degrees F (15.5 degrees C) in glass
Age when judged (since bottling): two months

Brewer's specifics

Mash grains at 155 degrees F (68.5 degrees C) for 60 minutes and sparge with 4 gallons of 170-degree-F (76.5-degree-C) water.

Judges' comments

"Needs a bit more hop aroma. A bit too estery. Excellent clarity and good head retention. Overall, very good."
"Fruity aroma; nice malt, not enough hops. Malt is missing in the flavor and body. The hops balance what malt is present, but would need to be increased to match what should be there. Could stand a touch more carbonation. Very slight oxidation."
"Nice hop and malt aroma. Appearance is good. Slightly more alelike flavor than appropriate for style. Overall a nice effort."

CHAPTER 22

WHEAT BEER

The unusual clove and sour flavor of wheat beer has to grow on you, but when it takes root, the flavor is hard to beat. Weisse beers have fairly high levels of lactic acid, and the sharp sourness is often tempered with raspberry syrup. These beers are highly attenuated and only slightly hopped. Weizen beers are characterized by a banana/clove character, which is primarily a yeast byproduct. Use a true wheat beer yeast when you brew these for a terrific summer-time quencher.

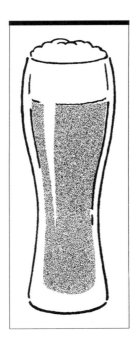

AHA National Homebrew Competition Style Guidelines

a) Berliner Weisse – Pale. Light body. Dry. Sharp lactic sourness. Fruity/estery. Between 60 and 70 percent malted wheat. Very low bitterness. No hop flavor or aroma. Effervescent. No diacetyl.

b) German-style Weizen/Weissbier – Pale to golden. Light to medium body. About 50 percent wheat malt. Clove and slight banana character. Fruity/estery. Clove, vanilla, nutmeg, smoke, and cinnamonlike phenolics permissible. Mild sourness OK. Highly effervescent. Cloudiness OK. Low bitterness. Low hop flavor and aroma OK. No diacetyl.

c) German-style Dunkelweizen – Deep copper to brown. Dark version of Weizen. Chocolatelike maltiness evident. Banana, cloves, and other phenolics may still be evident, but to a lesser degree. Stronger than Weizen. Medium body. Low diacetyl OK. Low hop flavor and aroma OK.

d) German-style Weizenbock – Usually deep copper to dark brown, but light versions can be amber to copper. Medium to full body. Alcoholic strength evident. Maltiness high. Low bitterness. Hop flavor and aroma absent. Banana and clove character apparent. Low diacetyl OK.

OG (Balling/Plato)	Percent alc./vol.	IBUs	SRM
a) Berliner Weisse			
1.028-32 (7-8)	2.8-3.4%	3-6	2-4
b) German-style Weizen/Weissbier			
1.048-56 (12-14)	4.8-5.4%	10-15	3-9
c) German-style Dunkelweizen (dark)			
1.048-56 (12-14)	4.8-5.4%	10-15	17-22
d) German-style Weizenbock			
1.066-80 (16.5-20)	6.5-7.5%	10-20	7-30

Supai's Weissbier

German-style Weizen/Weissbier
First Place, Wheat Beer, 1992
Eric Warner, Lafayette, Colorado
(all grain)

Ingredients for 10 gallons

10 1/3	pounds wheat malt
7	pounds pale barley malt
1/3	ounce Northern Brewer hops, 8 percent alpha acid (105 minutes)
1/4	ounce Hallertauer hops, 4.5 percent alpha acid (45 minutes)
1/4	ounce Hallertauer hops, 4.5 percent alpha acid (15 minutes)
	Yeast culture from bottle of German Moy Weissbier

Original specific gravity: 1.050
Final specific gravity: 1.012
Boiling time: 105 minutes
Primary fermentation: 10 days at 61 degrees F (16 degrees C) in open aluminum
Secondary fermentation: Seven days at 59 to 61 degrees F (15 to 16 degrees C) in bottle, 39 degrees F (4 degrees C) thereafter
Age when judged (since bottling): three months

Brewer's specifics

Single-decoction mash. Mash-in at 104 degrees F (40 degrees C) and heat to 122 degrees F (50 degrees C) for 25 minutes. Pull a decoction of about 40 percent of the mash volume. While maintaining the rest mash temperature, heat decoction to 160 degrees F (71 degrees C) for 15 minutes. Raise decoction temperature to boiling for 20 minutes. Mix the two mashes, adjust and hold temperature at 147 degrees F (64 degrees C) for 20 minutes, then raise temperature to 160 degrees F (71 degrees C) until conversion. Heat to 170 degrees F (77 degrees C) and sparge.

Judges' comments

"Soft, delicate cloviness and malt. Bitterness perfect. This is why I love wheat beers. Extraordinarily good."
"Nice effort. I like the fruitiness and clove combined with the carbonation."
"Good biting clove taste. Banana still hangs over the flavor profile, but this is only marginally detracting. A great drinking beer finishes clean but fruity. Could be more tart."
"Very nice flavor. Strong wheat flavor. Some vanilla. Could be more tart."

COLORADO WEIZEN

German-style Weizen/Weissbier
First Place, Wheat Beer, 1990
Michael Croddy, Colorado Springs, Colorado
(extract)

Ingredients for 5 gallons

6 2/3	*pounds American Brewmaster American Classic wheat malt extract*
1	*pound American Brewmaster malted rice extract*
2	*ounces Tettnanger hops (45 minutes)*
1	*ounce Tettnanger hops (one minute)*
4	*ounces maltodextrin*
	Wyeast No. 1028 British Ale liquid yeast
1/2	*cup corn sugar to prime*

Original specific gravity: 1.050
Final specific gravity: 1.010
Boiling time: 45 minutes
Primary fermentation: three days at 65 to 70 degrees F (18.5 to 21 degrees C) in glass
Secondary fermentation: 17 days at 65 to 70 degrees F (18.5 to 21 degrees C) in glass
Age when judged (since bottling): 2 1/2 months

Judges' comments

"Nice clovelike aroma. Nice color and clarity. Little head and it lacks retention. Distinct wheat flavor plus lots of clove. Very spicy, but well balanced. Medium bodied. Very nice example of German Weizen."

"Fruity aroma with a faint hint of cloves. Good color. Head retention is OK. Beer is slightly cloudy, but OK for category. Clove and green apple flavor. Malt comes through well. Hops are faint. Very good balance, good conditioning, very good fruity aftertaste. Full body, appropriate for style. Overall an excellent Weizen. Very drinkable. I love it."

"Nice wheat and hop aroma; a bit of sour aroma. Color and clarity are good. Not much head. Lovely wheat flavor. A little sour and sweet. Good hopping rate. Very drinkable. Fruity and sour tones in a wonderful combination."

Victory Beer Recipes

WEST COAST WHEAT

American Wheat Beer
Second Place, Wheat Beer, 1990
Ray Ballestero, Sacramento, California
(extract)

Ingredients for 5 gallons

6 1/2   pounds Weizenbier malt extract (60 percent wheat,
         40 percent barley)
1/4   ounce Northern Brewer hops (60 minutes)
1/3   ounce Nugget hops (30 minutes)
1/2   ounce Perle hops (dry)
         Brewer's Choice Bavarian Wheat liquid yeast

Original specific gravity: 1.036
Final specific gravity: 1.008
Boiling time: 60 minutes
Primary fermentation: six days at 60 degrees F (15.5 degrees C)
in glass
Secondary fermentation: one month at 60 degrees F (15.5
degrees C) in glass
Age when judged (since bottling): one month

Brewer's specifics

Naturally carbonated.

Judges' comments

"Nice aroma, some wheat. Very nice clear golden appearance.
Reminds me of a Millstream Wheat."
"Distinct clovelike aroma. Very nice, could be slightly fuller."
"Light body, but appropriate for style. Excellent brew overall. Could
drink a gallon — maybe more!"
"Very light wheaty aroma with a solventlike background. Good color
and clarity. Tight, creamy head leaves laces down the side of the
glass. Very clean and delicate with a light, wheaty taste. Extremely
light and clean wheat beer. Good effort!"

PALE MOON RIZEN WEIZEN

German-style Weizenbock
Second Place, Wheat Beer, 1991
Paddy Giffen, Cotati, California
(grain/extract)

Ingredients for 5 gallons

3 1/2	pounds amber dry malt extract
6	pounds wheat malt
3	pounds Klages malt
1 1/2	pounds 60 °L crystal malt
1 1/2	pounds CaraPils malt
1/2	ounce Perle hops (60 minutes)
1 1/4	ounces Saaz hops (30 minutes)
3/4	ounce Hallertauer hops (dry)
	Wyeast No. 3056 liquid yeast
2/3	cup corn sugar to prime

Original specific gravity: 1.074
Final specific gravity: 1.025
Boiling time: 60 minutes
Primary fermentation: five days at 65 degrees F (18 degrees C) in glass
Secondary fermentation: six weeks at 50 degrees F (10 degrees C) in glass
Age when judged (since bottling): 7 1/2 months

Brewer's specifics

Mash grains. Protein rest one-half hour at 120 degrees F (49 degrees C). Raise temperature to 152 degrees F (67 degrees C) for one-half hour, then raise to 157 degrees F (69.5 degrees C) for one-half hour.

Judges' comments

"Nice, warming Weizenbock. The alcohol level is appropriate."
"Great beer! Very enjoyable but could use more wheat character. Try a real Weizen yeast."
"This is a good-tasting, well-made, Weizen beer."

WEBSTER CLIFF WHEAT

Berliner Weisse
First Place, Wheat Beer, 1991
Mike Fertsch, Woburn, Massachusetts
(all grain)

Ingredients for 3 1/2 gallons

3 1/4	pounds Klages malt
3	pounds wheat malt
1/4	pound Munich malt
1/4	ounce Hallertauer hops, 4 percent alpha acid (60 minutes)
1/4	ounce Tettnanger hops, 4.5 percent alpha acid (40 minutes)
1/4	ounce Hallertauer hops, 4 percent alpha acid (40 minutes)
1/4	ounce Hallertauer hops, 4 percent alpha acid (20 minutes)
1/4	ounce Hallertauer hops, 4 percent alpha acid (one minute)
1/2	teaspoon gypsum in mash
1/2	teaspoon gypsum in sparge
	Cultured Stoudt Brewing Company wheat liquid yeast
1/2	cup corn sugar to prime

Original specific gravity: 1.046
Final specific gravity: 1.012
Boiling time: 60 minutes
Primary fermentation: six days at 65 degrees F (18.5 degrees C) in glass
Secondary fermentation: 15 days at 65 degrees F (18.5 degrees C) in glass
Age when judged (since bottling): five months

Brewer's specifics

Mash grains 90 minutes at 154 degrees F (68 degrees C).

Judges' comments

"Nice lactic sour nose, very appealing. Very light brew with a well-pronounced and accurate sourness. Slightly overbittered in finish. Very nice interpretation of style. Extremely refreshing beer!"

"Very appropriate lactic sour aroma. A bit too bitter. Sourness is just right. This is almost a perfect Weissbier. I must be in Berlin! Only flaw is a bit too much bitterness."

LACTIC WHEATIES

Berliner Weisse
Third Place, Wheat Beer, 1993
Bruce A. Brandt, Casnovia, Michigan
(all grain)

Ingredients for 5 1/2 gallons

3   pounds Ireks Pils malt
3   pounds Ireks wheat malt
0.42   ounce German Hersbrucker hops, 3.8 percent alpha
       acid (60 minutes)
       Yeast Lab Dusseldorf ale yeast culture, and
       Brettanomyces lambicus culture

Original specific gravity: 1.032
Final specific gravity: 1.008
Boiling time: 90 minutes
Primary fermentation: three days at 65 degrees F (18 degrees C) in glass
Secondary fermentation: 15 days at 75 degrees F (24 degrees C) in glass
Tertiary fermentation: 15 days at 32 degrees F (0 degrees C) in stainless steel
Age when judged (since bottling): two months

Brewer's specifics

Mash grains at 105 degrees F (41 degrees C) for 10 minutes. Raise to 122 degrees F (50 degrees C) for 30 minutes. Raise to 144 degrees F (62 degrees C) for 10 minutes. Raise to 148 degrees F (64 degrees C) for 20 minutes. Raise to 160 degrees F (71 degrees C) for 60 minutes. Raise to 168 degrees F (76 degrees C) for 10 minutes. Sparge with 4 1/2 gallons of 168-degree-F (76-degree-C) water.
Force carbonate and counter pressure bottle.

Judges' comments

"Good conditioning, nice tartness. Could even be a little more tart."
"Could be more acidic, crisp. Balance of malt and hops is good. Slight buttery aftertaste. Good try at a tough style."
"Smooth up front with nice lactic middle and finish. Seems right on the money to me. Very nice beer. Lactic sourness is quite evident."
"Just a little week on the acidity. Good aroma, good cloves."

CHAPTER 23

TRADITIONAL MEAD

Fermented honey was probably the first alcoholic beverage known to humankind. It has been know as the "drink of the gods" and is the origin of the word "honeymoon." For those who love to brew and drink it, mead still has mythological overtones, and remains one of the more simple beverages to brew: honey, water, yeast, and time are all that is needed. The flavors of mead are determined principally by the type of honey used, and by the residual sweetness of the finished product. Meads are famous for fermenting slowly, so be prepared to wait. It will be worth it!

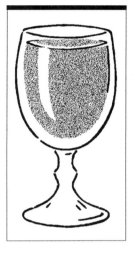

AHA National Homebrew Competition Style Guidelines

a) Sparkling – Effervescent. Dry, medium or sweet. Light to medium body. No flavors other than honey. Honey character in aroma and flavor. Low to fruity acidity. Color depends on honey type. Absence of harsh and stale character.

b) Still – Not effervescent. Dry, medium, sweet or very sweet. Light to full body. Honey character in aroma and flavor. Low to fruity acidity. Absence of harsh and stale character.

OG (Balling/Plato)	Percent alc./vol.	IBUs	SRM
a) Sparkling			
1.050-90 (12.5-22.5)	5-11%	0	0-4
b) Still			
1.090-1.140 (22.5-35)	11-15%	0	0-5

ALBERTA FROST

Sparkling
First Place, Traditional Mead, 1992
Byron Burch, Santa Rosa, California
1992 Meadmaker of the Year

Ingredients for 5 gallons

12	pounds Meadmakers Magic™ Canadian Clover Honey
4	ounces tartaric acid
2	ounces The Beverage People™ yeast nutrient for meads
1/4	teaspoon The Beverage People™ Irish moss
20	grams The Beverage People™ Prise de Mousse wine yeast
	The Beverage People™ liquid oak extract to taste
	(approximately 25 mL)

Original specific gravity: 1.080
Final specific gravity: 1.010
Primary fermentation: seven days at 80 degrees F (27 degrees C) in glass
Secondary fermentation: 21 days at 80 degrees F (27 degrees C) in glass
Age when judged (since bottling): nine months

Judges' comments

"Slightly sweet flavor and good fizz. Finishes with nice citrus balance, sweet and tart."
"Nice."
"No obvious problems. Balanced by slight acid in finish."
"Robust complex flavor, tart and sweet, melonlike in the middle. Nice mouthfeel."

FULL MOON MEAD

Still
First Place, Traditional Mead, 1989
Wayne Waananen, Denver, Colorado

Ingredients for 5 gallons

10	pounds Sue Bee clover honey
2	pounds home-grown wild honey
4	teaspoons acid blend
5	teaspoons yeast nutrient
2	packets Red Star Champagne yeast

Original specific gravity: 1.094
Final specific gravity: 1.010
Boiling time: 30 minutes
Primary fermentation: 10 months at 62 degrees F (16.5 degrees C) in glass
Secondary fermentation: yes (duration not given) in stainless steel
Age when judged (since bottling): 1 1/2 months

Judges' comments

"Nice honey aroma with a hint of fruit. Very slight haze. Honey flavor is great. Was this citrus honey? Slightly phenolic but not bad. Good still mead. Delicate!"

"Very floral, honeyish aroma a little yeasty (breadlike). Extremely light appearance. Flavor is a bit on the acidic side, but all right. Overall a very nice and clean entry. A bit fruity in character from acidity. Delicate."

OH HONEY, LET IT BE MEAD!

Sparkling
Third Place, Traditional Mead, 1991
Philip Fleming, Broomfield, Colorado

Ingredients for 5 gallons

12	pounds Madhava honey
1/2	teaspoon gypsum
5	teaspoons acid blend
1	teaspoon Irish moss
	Lalvin EC-1118 Prisse de Mousse liquid culture
5	teaspoons yeast nutrient
1	cup corn sugar to prime

Original specific gravity: 1.074
Final specific gravity: 1.003
Boiling time: 30 minutes
Primary fermentation: 21 days at 67 degrees F (19.5 degrees C) in glass
Secondary fermentation: 35 days at 65 degrees F (18. 5 degrees C) in glass
Age when judged (since bottling): 16 months

Judges' comments

"Honey flavor not intense, relatively dry, slightly sharp. Body a little thin but not unusual for sparkling mead. Finish fades. Could use a little more honey flavor and less acidity. Appearance very good."

"Excellent balance. Very clean and well-conditioned. Leaves a nice warming sensation making you want to have another sip."

"Excellent. Clean with just a hint of hotness on the tongue. Good carbonation. Balanced. Could have slightly more body."

SACK MEAD

Still
First Place, Traditional Mead, 1990
Gordon Olson, Los Alamos, New Mexico

Ingredients for 5 1/2 gallons

15	pounds Grade A fancy honey
1/2	teaspoon Irish moss
4	teaspoons acid blend
6	teaspoons yeast nutrient
2	packets Red Star Champagne yeast

Original specific gravity: 1.110
Final specific gravity: 1.016
Primary fermentation: six months at 65 to 75 degrees F (18.5 to 24 degrees C) in glass
Age when judged (since bottling): 10 1/2 months

Judges' comments

"Strong sweet honey aroma, very inviting. Pale yellow color; clear. Sweet start, strong honey flavor, smooth gradually drying finish, nice alcohol warmth. Very nice. Strong sweet honey character but not cloying or lingering."

"Aroma is very heavy. Nice. Excellent color and clarity. Very good-looking sample! Flavor is excellent. Very slight carbonation combines with acidity for nice, sharp aftertaste."

"Wonderful honey aroma; strong alcohol. Clear for having sediment. Small bubbles at bottom of glass. Wonderful traditional flavor, strong alcohol, sweet. Carbonation exists, but slight. Great mead!"

CHAPTER 24

FLAVORED MEAD

Flavored meads are just like traditional meads except fruit and herbs are used as adjuncts to alter the flavor. There are six principal versions of flavored mead: Melomel is made with fruit other than grapes or apples, Cyser is made with apples or apple juice, Pyment is made with grapes or grape juice, Metheglin uses herbs and/or spices, Hippocras is Pyment with spices, and Braggot is made with malted barley and sometimes hops.

AHA National Homebrew Competition Style Guidelines

a) Sparkling – Effervescent and made with any fruit, apple juice, grapes, herbs, or spices. Flavors should be expressed in aroma and flavor. Color should represent ingredients. Light to medium body. Dry, medium, or sweet. Honey character still apparent in aroma and flavor. Absence of harsh and stale character.

b) Still – Not effervescent. Made with any fruit, apple juice, grapes, herbs, or spices. Flavors should be expressed in aroma and flavor. Color should represent ingredients. Light to full body. Dry, medium, sweet, or very sweet. Honey character apparent in aroma and flavor. Absence of harsh and stale character.

OG (Balling/Plato)	Percent alc./vol.	IBUs	SRM
a) Sparkling			
1.050-90 (12.5-22.5)	5-11%	0-15	0-?
b) Still			
1.090-1.140 (22.5-35)	11-15%	0-20	0-?

AFTERGLOW

Still
Second Place, Melomel, Cyser, Pyment, Metheglin, 1991
David Sherfey, La Crescenta, California

Ingredients for 1 gallon

3 4/5	pounds clover honey
4 1/2	grams yeast nutrient
1/16	teaspoon sodium metabisulfite
5	grams Red Star Prisse de Mousse yeast
1	Pasilla chili
1	New Mexican chili
1	Californian chili
1	tiny round "hot mama" chili

Original specific gravity: 1.130
Final specific gravity: 1.032
Primary fermentation: not given
Secondary fermentation: not given
Age when judged (since bottling): not given

Brewer's specifics

Mix honey with 1 quart of 80-degree-F (27-degree-C) water.
Mix yeast nutrient and sodium metabisulfite in one-half cup
water. Pour all ingredients into 1-gallon fermenter and top off
with enough water to make 1 gallon. Let stand for two days
then pitch yeast. When fermentation stops, rack off the yeast.
Deseed and chop the chilies and dry hop to taste in a sterile
straining bag.

Judges' comments

"Wonderful! Nice blend of chilies and just right in volume."
"Good. Not too hot. No off-flavors, not too fiery."
"Both the honey and chilies come through. Very finely-crafted mead,
balancing all the flavors. Very nice. Would be great with food!"

APRICOT APHRODISIAC

Sparkling
Third Place, Melomel Cyser, Pyment, Metheglin, 1989
Joseph Hauge, Portland, Oregon

Ingredients for 5 1/2 gallons

7	pounds light honey
1 1/4	pounds corn sugar
1	ounce Cascade hop pellets (60 minutes)
5	ounces chopped ginger root
1 1/2	ounces Spanish lemon zest
1 1/2	ounces lemon grass
2	pounds pitted crushed apricots (10 minutes)
1 1/2	ounces gypsum
1	packet Red Star California Champagne yeast
2/3	cup corn sugar to prime

Original specific gravity: 1.065
Final specific gravity: 1.005
Boiling time: 60 minutes
Primary fermentation: five weeks at 65 degress F (18.5 degrees C) in glass
Secondary fermentation: four weeks at 65 degrees F (18.5 degrees C) in glass
Age when judged (since bottling): 4 1/2 months

Brewer's specifics
Ginger root, lemon peel, and lemon grass put in for whole boil. Rough sparge to primary. Carefully strain with a fine screen when racking to secondary.

Judges' comments
"Apricot noticeable in front, strong lemon follows, honey somewhat hidden. Very small particles and slight haze. Honey comes through first followed by apricot, and sour-tart lemon taste. Very good. Lemon overdone slightly, shows in aftertaste. Great sweetness."

"Great candy-lemon nose. Great color and head! Although I don't taste much apricot, it adds to the candy palate. Overall, real nice. Try for less acidity."

"Wow, lemon and apricot aromas are excellent. Appearance is a bit hazy but not serious. Nice sweetness. Well-balanced. Wonderful job. Gentle flavors are all discernable. This is a nice sparkling mead. Good job of keeping sweetness in a sparkling mead. I think your secret is in the yeast."

NOGALES MEAD

Still
First Place, Melomel, Cyser, Pyment, Metheglin, 1989
Shelby Meyer, Tucson, Arizona
1989 Meadmaker of the Year

Ingredients for 2 gallons

8	pounds Malcom's Desert Mesquite honey
3/4	ounce black walnut leaves
2	teaspoons L.D. Carlson yeast nutrient
2	teaspoons L.D. Carlson acid blend
1/20	ounce Prise de Mousse Champagne yeast

Original specific gravity: not given
Final specific gravity: not given
Boiling time: 20 minutes
Primary fermentation: 18 weeks in glass
Secondary fermentation: 16 weeks in glass
Age when judged (since bottling): 13 months

Judges' comments

"Honey notes are evident in aroma; slight smokiness with higher alcohols. Nice, slightly brown-gold color; great clarity. Great honey flavor! Sweetness helps mask tannins; slightly bitter aftertaste. Alcoholic! Great mead. Lay it down and it will improve."

"Smells like airplane glue. Higher alcohols from high temperature fermentation? Deep golden color. Nice, sweet, full flavor. Fusel alcohols from high-temperature fermentation? Recipe is exceptionally nice. Maybe change yeast or keep temperature between 70 and 75 degrees F (21 and 24 degrees C)."

RASPBERRY

Sparkling
First Place, Melomel, Cyser, Pyment, Metheglin, 1990
John McKew and Graca Vicente, Davis, California
1990 Meadmakers of the Year

Ingredients for 5 gallons

14	pounds orange blossom honey
5	pounds raspberries
2 1/2	pounds blueberries
	Red Star Champagne yeast
	corn sugar to prime

Original specific gravity: 1.083
Final specific gravity: 1.017
Primary fermentation: three months at 85 degrees F (29.5 degrees C) in glass
Age when judged (since bottling): two years, seven months

Brewers' specifics

Pasteurize honey and 1 gallon of water by keeping at 176 degrees F (80 degrees C) for one-half hour. Pasteurize berries by heating to 176 to 194 degrees F (80 to 90 degrees C). Mix, cool, and pitch yeast.

Judges' comments

"Nice raspberry-blueberry nose with some orange blossom-type honey — lots of honey. Dark amber color; should be reddish-blue. Clear with nice bubbles and legs. Flavor is sweet but not too sweet, and has nice raspberry, blueberry, and honey characteristics. Slight astringency; carbonation is good. Very drinkable; great balance of fruit and honey. Awesome mead. Keep up the good work."
"Nice fruit aroma. Nice clarity and color. Nice honey flavor. Raspberries and blueberries blend nicely."
"Great fruit aroma; good alcohol nose. Good color, tight bead. Flavor has a good balance of fruit and honey, good carbonation. Excellent. Overall a great balance. Slight bitterness in finish."

JOHNSTOWN BREWING GINGER MEAD

Sparkling
First Place, Melomel, Cyser, Pyment, Metheglin, 1991
Steven Yuhas and Ed Gilles, Windber, Pennsylvania
1991 Meadmakers of the Year

Ingredients for 5 gallons

12	pounds wildflower honey
1	ounce Saaz hops (one minute)
1	teaspoon citric acid
2 1/2	ounces ginger root
1/4	teaspoon Irish moss
3	teaspoons yeast nutrient
	Red Star dry ale yeast
1/2	cup corn sugar to prime, boiled with a little mead

Original specific gravity: 1.088
Final specific gravity: 1.023
Boiling time: 60 minutes
Primary fermentation: seven days at 65 degrees F (18.5 degrees C) in glass
Secondary fermentation: 39 days at 65 degrees F (18.5 degrees C) in glass
Age when judged (since bottling): two months

Brewers' specifics

Honey used was unprocessed, Triple Grade A, western Pennsylvania, fall wildflower honey. Boil ginger one hour in must.

Judges' comments

"Great wildflower comes through flavor with candylike ginger. A real ace!"
"Appropriate acidity and sweetness. Ginger comes through, but could be more intense. I love this mead!"
"Full ginger, medium-full honey in aroma. Good balance between honey and aromatics, but not too much ginger. Good!"

LIME MEAD

Still
Third Place, Melomel, Cyser, Pyment, Metheglin, 1993
Peter Knight, St. Helena, California

Ingredients for 4 gallons
15   pounds honey
6   ounces lime juice
        Prise de Mousse wine yeast

Original specific gravity: 1.140
Final specific gravity: 1.020
Boiling time: 10 minutes
Primary fermentation: two months at 70 degrees F (21 degrees C) in glass
Secondary fermentation: four months at 70 degrees F (21 degrees C) in glass
Age when judged (since bottling): 13 months

Judges' comments
"Lime juice comes through with good honey beneath. On the verge of cloying, but lime cuts this down a bit. Had to search a bit for honey in aroma."
"Sweet. Some lime. A little acidic. Maybe needs more lime. A little sweet."
"Light sweetness. Light acid in finish. Very clean. Nice sour character in flavor."
"Sweetness has a uniqueness about it. Good clean finish and good balance."

CHAPTER 25

CIDER

One of the all-time classic fermented beverages, cider is a refreshing drink any time of year. For the best cider, use the freshest apples or apple juice you can find, and pay close attention to the varieties. Tart and sweet apples produce ciders of widely different characteristics, and some brewers blend the juice of different varieties to produce a desired result. Making cider is simple, and the final product is absolutely fabulous.

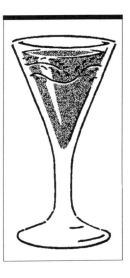

AHA National Homebrew Competition Style Guidelines

a) Still – Not effervescent. Less than 7 percent alcohol by volume. Can be dry or sweet. Pale yellow color, must be clear or brilliant. Apple aroma. Light bodied and crisp apple flavor. Sugar adjuncts may be used.

b) Sparkling – Effervescent but not foamy. May be force carbonated. No head. Less than 8 percent alcohol by volume. Dry or sweet. Pale yellow color, must be clear and brilliant. Light to medium body, crisp apple taste. Sugar adjuncts may be used.

c) New England-style – Still or sparkling dry cider. Carbonation must be natural. Between 8 and 14 percent alcohol. Pale to medium yellow color. Pronounced apple aroma. Medium to full body. Balanced by drying tannins, but never hot due to excess alcohol. Adjuncts include white and brown sugars, molasses, or raisins. Wild or wine yeasts only.

d) Specialty Cider – Any and all adjuncts and yeasts may be used. Alcohol content must be below 14 percent. At least 75 percent apple juice must be used in the must.

OG (Balling/Plato)	Percent alc./vol.	IBUs	SRM
a) Still			
1.045-53	7%	—	—
b) Sparkling			
1.045-61	8%	—	—
c) New England-style			
1.061-105	8-14%	—	—
d) Specialty Cider			
1.045-105	5.8-14%	—	—

Sparkling
First Place, Cider, 1992
Charles Castellow, Edmonds, Washington
1992 Cidermaker of the Year

Ingredients for 3 gallons

3	gallons apple cider
	Vintners' Choice Pasteur Champagne yeast
3	ounces lactose
28	ounces frozen apple juice concentrate

Original specific gravity: not given
Final specific gravity: 1.004
Primary fermentation: 21 days at 68 degrees F (20 degrees C) in glass
Age when judged (since bottling): three months

Brewer's specifics

Lactose and apple juice concentrate added after kegging.

Judges' comments

"Very pretty with an appley, light aroma. A little too sweet in the balance, but very drinkable."
"Smooth, soft, banana flavors. Low acid and tannins. Nice."
"Lovely brilliant yellow-orange color. Creamy and well balanced. A touch sweet but well balanced."

STILL #1

Still
First Place, Cider, 1993
Gabriel Ostriker
1993 Cidermaker of the Year, Somerville, Massachussetts

Ingredients for 5 gallons

5 gal	blended apple juices
	Wild yeast
5	Campden tablets
	Sugar

Original specific gravity: 1.055
Final specific gravity: 1.005
Primary fermentation: one month at 60 degrees F (16 degrees C) in plastic
Age when judged (since bottling): not given

Brewers specifics

Natural yeast from apples will ferment under a fermentation lock. Add Campden tablets (1 per gallon of juice) at beginning of primary fermentation. Add enough suger to raise the original specific gravity of the juice to 1.055.

Judges' comments

"Very clear, no sediment. Nice apple aroma. Good color. Body could be a bit bigger, but it is very nice. Nice sweet flavor balanced well with acidity. Nice aftertaste. Great job. Makes you want to drink more."
"Good fill with no sediment. Apply nose. Brilliant pale yellow. Well-balanced. Slightly thin-bodied, but not a big flaw. Very good cider. Slightly sweet, would be good with dessert."

CHAPTER 26

SAKÉ

Saké is a highly unusual fermented beverage. Using special rice molds, this ancient brew actually converts starch into sugar at the same time it is producing alcohol and carbon dioxide. Many people assume saké is a wine, but because it's made from a cereal grain it is technically beer. It has the highest alcohol content of any naturally fermented brew, sometimes more than 20 percent by volume. It can be served warmed, chilled, over ice, and even in mixed drinks such as a saké martini. It's great with a lemon twist, and of course, is a requirement with Asian cuisine.

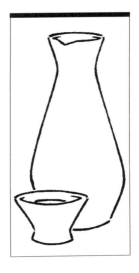

AHA National Homebrew Competition Style Guidelines

a) Saké (Japanese Rice Beer) – Twelve to 20 percent alcohol. Can be semidry to very dry. No carbonation. Pale yellow color to almost water clarity. Must be made with rice koji, rice, and yeast only. This subcategory includes Genshu saké, ordinary saké, Nigori saké, Ginjo saké, brown rice (Genmai) saké, rice wine, and fruit saké.

b) Sparkling Saké – This is regular saké refermented in the bottle (like Champagne) to produce carbonation. It is about 12.5 percent alcohol, and the bottle priming is rice syrup and yeast. Can be made from fruit saké.

c) Other Oriental Rice Beers – This subcategory includes Chinese amber rice beer (Huang-Chiu), Korean saké types (Taek Ju and other Jus), saké variations from other grains (corn, barley, millet, etc.), and Mirin (cooking) saké .

OG (Balling/Plato)	Percent alc./vol.	IBUs	SRM
a) Saké (Japanese rice beer)			
—	12-20%	—	—
b) Sparkling Saké			
—	12.5%	—	—
c) Other Oriental Rice Beers			
— varies with style	—		—

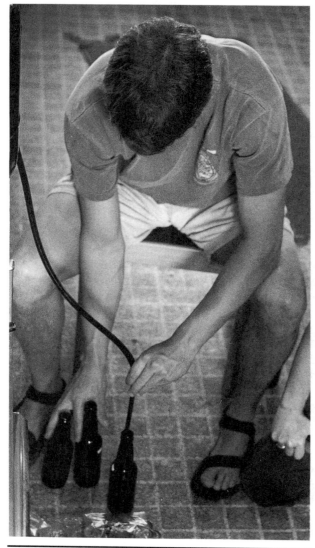

SAKÉ LITE

Saké (Japanese Rice Beer)
First Place, Saké, 1992
Tina Long, Sacramento, California
1992 Sakémaker of the Year

Ingredients for 3 gallons
10	*pounds short-grain rice*
2 1/2	*pounds rice koji*
2	*gallons, 20 ounces water*
3/5	*teaspoon wine yeast nutrient*
1 1/4	*teaspoon Morton salt substitute*
1	*package Red Star sherry yeast*
1	*package finings*

Brewer's specifics
This recipe is by Fred Eckhardt. Eckhardt uses three steps: moto (yeast mash), moromi (main ferment), and yodan (stabilizing step). In the moto step, a "yeast starter" is made and gradually built up during the moromi step with three additions of rice, water, and koji over a four-day period. Yodan is a final addition of water that adjusts the alcohol content of the saké. A secondary ferment is used to mature the final product.

Judges' comments
"Very good."
"No real off-flavors."
"Good body."
"Give me a liter and some sushi and I'll be happy all night. Excellent."
"Polishing rice is best. Good saké."

ICHIBAN

Saké (Japanese Rice Beer)
First Place, Saké, 1993
Jim Long, Sacramento, California
1993 Sakémaker of the Year

Ingredients for 3 gallons

10	pounds short-grain rice
2 1/2	pounds rice koji
2	gallons, 20 ounces of water
3/5	teaspoon wine yeast nutrient
1 1/4	teaspoon Morton salt substitute
	Yeast culture from Hakusan Sake, Napa, California
1	package finings

Brewer's specifics

Standard saké brewing uses three steps: moto (yeast mash), moromi (main ferment) and yodan (stabilizing step). In the moto step, a "yeast starter" is made and then gradually built up dring the moromi step with three additions of rice, water, and koji over a four-day period. Yodan is a final addition of water that adjusts the alcohol content of the saké . A secondary ferment is used to mature the final product.

Judges' comments

"Excellent balance. More dry than medium. Smooth. Yummy yummy. Slightly acidic but much lower acidity than any others I've tried."

"By far the best. Delicate. Good clean nose, no heavy acidity."

"Excellent flavor. Good balance. Very pleasant."

APPENDICIES

FOR ADDITIONAL INFORMATION

Here are several additional sources of information to help you expand your knowledge of homebrewing. These are some of the best books and articles we know of to help you make and perfect the brews covered in this book, as well as the ones you create yourself.

For more information on these books and articles, or to find out more about homebrewing, contact the American Homebrewers Association at PO Box Boulder, CO 80306-1679; or call (303) 447-0816.

American Mead Association, PO Box 4666, Grand Junction, CO 81502.

Art of Cidermaking, The by Paul Correnty, Brewers Publications, to be released 1995.

Beer Companion by Michael Jackson, Running Press, 1993.

Belgian Ale by Pierre Rajotte, Brewers Publications, 1992.

Bock by Darryl Richman, Brewers Publications, 1994.

Brewers and Their Gadgets, **zymurgy** Special Issue 1988, American Homebrewers Association.

Brewing Lager Beer by Greg Noonan, Brewers Publications, 1986.

Brewing Mead by Colonel Robert Gayre with Charlie Papazian, Brewers Publications, 1986.

Brewing Process, The, **zymurgy** Special Issue 1992, American Homebrewers Association.

Brewing the World's Great Beers by David Miller, Storey Publishing, 1992.

Continental Pilsener by David Miller, Brewers Publications, 1990.

Dictionary of Beer and Brewing by Carl Forget, Brewers Publications, 1988.

Essentials of Beer Style, The, by Fred Eckhardt, Fred Eckhardt Associates Inc., 1989.

German Wheat Beer by Eric Warner, Brewers Publications, 1992.

Historical Companion to House-Brewing, The by Clive La Pensée, Montag Publications, 1990.

Hops and Beer, **zymurgy** Special Issue 1990, American Homebrewers Association.

Lambic by Jean-Xavier Guinard, Brewers Publications, 1990.

New Complete Joy of Home Brewing, The by Charlie Papazian, Avon Books, 1991.

Pale Ale by Terry Foster, Brewers Publications, 1990.

Porter by Terry Foster, Brewers Publications, 1991.

Practical Brewer, The, The Master Brewers Association of the Americas, 1977.

Saké Connection, The, PO Box 546, Portland, OR 97207.

"Saké - Japanese Rice Wine," **zymurgy**, Fall 1982 (Vol. 5, No. 3.)

Sake (U.S.A.) by Fred Eckhardt, Fred Eckhardt Communications, 1992.

Scotch Ale by Greg Noonan, Brewers Publications, 1993.

"Simple Math and Your Homebrew," **zymurgy**, Spring 1992 (Vol. 15 No. 3.)

Sweet and Hard Cider by Annie Proulx and Lew Nichols, Garden Way, 1980.

Traditional Beer Styles, **zymurgy** Special Issue 1991, American Homebrewers Association.

Traditional German, British and American Brewing Methods, **zymurgy** Special Issue 1993, American Homebrewers Association.

Troubleshooting, **zymurgy** Special Issue 1987, American Homebrewers Association.

AMERICAN HOMEBREWERS ASSOCIATION AWARD WINNERS

AHA HOMEBREWER OF THE YEAR

In the American Homebrewers Association National Homebrew Competition, the first-place beers in each category are judged in a best-of-show judging. The brewer of the winning beer is named Homebrewer of the Year. The winners of the Homebrewer of the Year award for the past 15 years are listed here.

1979 Tim Mead, Boulder, Colorado
1980 Mary Beth Millard-Bassett, Turner, Oregon
1981 Dave Miller, St. Louis, Missouri
1982 Don Thompson, Plano, Texas
1983 Nancy Vineyard, Santa Rosa, California
1984 Dewayne Lee Saxton, Chico, California
1985 Russ Schehrer, Denver, Colorado
1986 Byron Burch, Santa Rosa, California
1987 Ray Spangler, Erlanger, Kentucky
1988 John Maier, Juneau, Alaska
1989 Paul Prozeller, Hamden, Connecticut
1990 Richard Schmit, Arlington Heights, Illinois
1991 James Post, Newtown, Connecticut
1992 Stu Tallman, Rochester, Massachusetts
1993 Paddy Giffen, Cotati, California

AHA MEADMAKER OF THE YEAR

In the American Homebrewers Association National Homebrew Competition, the first-place meads in each category are judged in a best-of-show judging. The brewer of the winning mead is named Meadmaker of the Year. The following are the winners of the Meadmaker of the Year award.

1981 Roger Haynes, Thousand Oaks, California
1982 Ben Edmundson, Memphis, Tennessee
1983 Robert Townley, Westminster, Colorado
1984 Earl Koster, Westminster, Colorado
1985 Bill Pfeiffer, Wyandotte, Michigan
1986 John Montgomery, Bryan, Texas
1987 Kerry Carpenter, Baker, Oregon
1988 Ralph Bucca, District Heights, Maryland
1989 Shelby Meyer, Tucson, Arizona
1990 John McKew, Davis, California
1991 Steven Yuhas and Ed Gilles, Windber, Pennsylvania
1992 Byron Burch, Santa Rosa, California
1993 Walter Dobrowney, Saskatoon, Saskatchewan, Canada

AHA CIDERMAKER OF THE YEAR

The first-place cider brewer is awarded Cidermaker of the Year. In 1992 the award was given for the first time.

1992 Charles Castellow, Edmonds, Washington
1993 Gabriel Ostriker, Somerville, Massachusetts

AHA SAKÉMAKER OF THE YEAR

The first-place saké brewer is awarded Sakémaker of the Year. In 1992 the award was given for the first time.

1992 Tina Long, Sacramento, California
1993 Jim Long, Sacramento, California

AHA NINKASI AWARD WINNER

Points are given to a brewer for placing in the National Homebrew Competition. Three points are given for a first place, two points for a second place, and one point for a third place. The brewer accumulating the most points is named Ninkasi brewer. The 1992 award was the first.

1992 Steven J. and Christina Daniel, League City, Texas
1993 Walter Dobrowney, Saskatoon, Saskatchewan, Canada

FORMULAS AND CONVERSIONS

Here are some basic ways of calculating how these recipes will work for you. This information is by no means detailed, so be sure to research other sources for more information on recipe formulation techniques.

Bittering Units

For a one-hour boil, percent utilization is usually 25 to 30. The constant that converts these formulas from metric to U.S. units is 1.34.

$$IBU = \frac{(ounces\ of\ hops \times \%\ alpha\ acid\ of\ hops \times \%\ utilization)}{(gallons \times 1.34)}$$

$$HBU = \frac{(IBU \times gallons \times 1.34)}{\%\ utilization}$$

Homebrew Bittering Units are a measure of the total amount of bitterness in a given volume of beer. Bittering units can easily be calculated by multiplying the percent of alpha acid in the hops by the number of ounces. For example, if 2 ounces of Northern Brewer hops (9 percent alpha acid) and 3 ounces of Cascade hops (5 percent alpha acid) were used in a 10-gallon batch, the total amount of bittering units would be 33: (2 x 9) + (3 x 5) = 18 + 15. Bittering units per gallon would be 3.3 in a 10-gallon batch or 6.6 in a 5-gallon batch, so it is important to note volumes whenever expressing bittering units.

Alcohol Content

Alcohol by weight = (Original Gravity - Final Gravity) x 105
Alcohol by volume = Alcohol by weight x 1.25
Alcohol by weight = Alcohol by volume x 0.80
For example, the original gravity of your beer was 1.060, the final gravity is 1.015. So, the equation reads (1.060-1.015) x 105 = 4.7% alcohol by weight. Alcohol by volume = 4.7 x 1.25, which is 5.9% alcohol by volume.

Using Dry Malt Extract and Malt Extract Syrup

Malt extract syrup is 15 to 18 percent water. Therefore, the amount of dry extract to use in a recipe calling for extract syrup is about 85 percent of the quantity of syrup given in the recipe. Use the following two formulas to convert extract recipes from one type of extract to the other.

Amount of Liquid Extract Given x 0.85 = Amount of Dry Extract to Use
Amount of Dry Extract Given ÷ 0.85 = Amount of Liquid Extract to Use

---

Converting an All-Grain Recipe to Extract

The amount of extract to substitute in a recipe using all grain is about 75 percent of the amount of grain given in the recipe. Use the following two formulas to convert between extract recipes and all-grain recipes.

Amount of Grain Given x 0.75 = Amount of Extract to Use
Amount of Extract Given ÷ 0.75 = Amount of Grain to Use

Note that "grain" in these formulas refers the grain that will provide the fermentable constituents in your wort. They won't work for converting specialty grains to extract.

Estimating Original Gravity

$$\text{Pounds of malt needed} = \frac{(OG - 1) \times \text{number of gallons}}{(\text{extraction rating} - 1)}$$

For example, you want to brew 5 gallons of an Oktoberfest beer, with an original gravity of about 1.054. You know your extraction rating is about 1.025, so the equation reads: (1.054-1) x 5÷(1.025-1) = 10.8 pounds of malt for your batch. The extraction rating of a malt is the specific gravity of one gallon of wort made from one pound of the malt. Extraction ratings, therefore, can vary according to the kind of malt you use. A malt extract syrup will have a rating of about 1.033, dried malt about 1.038 to 1.042, Vienna malt about 1.025, etc. You can often find out these ratings at your homebrew supply shop.

Your extraction rating varies according to your brewing system and the type of malt being used.

Estimating Color

(pounds of malt A x color rating of malt A) + (pounds of malt B x color rating of malt B) + ... = (gallons of beer) x (color of beer)

For example, if you are brewing 5 gallons of beer with a desired color rating of 12, the right side of the equation equals 60. By substituting the color ratings and weights for the malts you want to use, you can figure out how much of each malt will give you the desired color. For instance, Munich malt has a color rating of 10 and Vienna malt has a color rating of 4. So it will take 7 1/2 pounds of Vienna malt and 3 pounds of Munich malt to give you a color rating of 12 in your finished beer. Your homebrew supply shop should be able to give you color values for the malts you purchase. Different malts have different color ratings.For more details, check *zymurgy* Spring 1992 (Vol. 15, No. 1).

American Homebrewers Association
1994 National Homebrew Competition

STYLE GUIDELINES CHART

The following is the 1994 American Homebrewers Association's style guidelines chart. The guidelines chart is updated annually and used in homebrew competitions. For more information on the National Homebrew Competition, Beer Judge Certification Program, or Sanctioned Competition Program, call or write the American Homebrewers Association, PO Box 1679, Boulder, CO, 80306-1679, (303) 447-0816, FAX (303) 447-2825.

ALE

		Original Gravity (Balling/Plato)	Percent Alc./Vol.	Int'l Bittering Units	Color SRM
1.	**Barley Wine**				
a)	Barley Wine	1.090-1.120 (22.5-30)	8.4-12%	50-100	14-22
2.	**Belgian and French Ale**				
a)	Flanders Brown	1.045-56 (11-14)	4.8-5.2%	15-25	10-20
b)	Dubbel	1.050-70 (12.5-17.5)	6-7.5%	18-25	10-14
c)	Tripel	1.070-95 (17.5-24)	7-10%	20-25	3.5-5.5
d)	Belgian Ale	1.044-54 (11-13.5)	4-6%	20-30	3.5-12
e)	Belgian Strong Ale	1.063-95 (16-24)	7-12%	20-50	3.5-20
f)	White	1.044-50 (11-12.5)	4.5-5.2%	15-25	2-4
g)	Bière de Garde	1.060-80 (15-20)*	4.5-8%	25-30	8-12
3.	**Belgian-style Lambic**				
a)	Faro	1.044-56 (11-14)	5-6%	11-23	6-15
b)	Gueuze	1.044-56 (11-14)	5-6%	11-23	6-13
c)	Fruit (Framboise,Kriek, Etc.)	1.040-72 (10-17.5)	5-7%	15-21	—
4.	**Brown Ale**				
a)	English Brown	1.040-50 (10-12.5)	4.5-5%	15-25	15-22
b)	English Mild	1.032-36 (8-9)	2.5-3.6%	14-20	17-34
c)	American Brown	1.040-55 (10-14)	4-5.5%	25-60	15-22
5.	**English-style Pale Ale**				
a)	Classic English Pale Ale	1.044-56 (11-14)	4.5-5.5%	20-40	4-11
b)	India Pale Ale	1.050-65 (12.5-15)	5-6.5%	40-65	8-14
6.	**American-style Ale**				
a)	American Pale Ale	1.044-56 (11-14)	4.5-5.5%	20-40	4-11
b)	American Wheat	1.030-50 (7.5-12.5)	4.3-5.5%	5-17	2-8
7.	**English Bitter**				
a)	English Ordinary	1.035-38 (8.5-9.5)	3-3.5%	20-25	8-12
b)	English Special	1.038-42 (9.5-10.5)	3.5-4.5%	25-30	12-14
c)	English Extra Special	1.042-55 (10.5-13.5)	4.5-6%	30-35	12-14
8.	**Scottish Ale**				
a)	Scottish Light	1.030-35 (7.5-9)	3-4%	9-15	8-17
b)	Scottish Heavy	1.035-40 (9-10)	3.5-4%	12-17	10-19
c)	Scottish Export	1.040-50 (10-12.5)	4-4.5%	15-20	10-19
9.	**Porter**				
a)	Robust Porter	1.044-60 (11-15)	5-6.5%	25-40	30+
b)	Brown Porter	1.040-50 (10-12.5)	4.5-6%	20-30	20-35
10.	**English and Scottish Strong Ale**				
a)	English Old Ale/Strong Ale	1.060-75 (15-19)	6.5-8.5%	30-40	10-16
b)	Strong "Scotch" Ale	1.072-85 (18-21)	6.2-8%	25-35	10-47
11.	**Stout**				
a)	Classic Dry Stout	1.038-48 (9.5-12)	3.8-5%	30-40	40+
b)	Foreign-style	1.052-72 (13-18)	6-7.5%	30-60	40+
c)	Sweet Stout	1.045-56 (11-14)	3-6%	15-25	40+
d)	Imperial Stout	1.075-95 (19-23.5)	7-9%	50-80	20+

LAGER

		Original Gravity (Balling/Plato)	Percent Alc./Vol.	Int'l Bittering Units	Color SRM
12.	**Bock**				
a)	Traditional German Bock	1.066-74 (16.5-18.5)	6-7.5%	20-30	20-30
b)	Helles (light) Bock	1.066-68 (16.5-17)	6-7.5%	20-35	4.5-6
c)	Doppelbock	1.074-80 (18.5-20)	6.5-8%	17-27	12-30
d)	Eisbock	1.092-1.116 (23-29)	8.6-14.4%	26-33	18-50
13.	**Bavarian Dark**				
a)	Munich Dunkel	1.052-56 (13-14)	4.5-5%	16-25	17-23
b)	Schwarzbier	1.044-52 (11-13)	3.8-5%	22-30	25-30
14.	**German Light Lager**				
a)	Dortmund/Export	1.048-56 (12-14)	4.8-6%	23-29	4-6
b)	Munich Helles	1.044-52 (11-13)	4.5-5.5%	18-25	3-5

STYLE GUIDELINES CHART

The following is the 1994 American Homebrewers Association's style guidelines chart. The guidelines chart is updated annually and used in homebrew competitions. For more information on the National Homebrew Competition, Beer Judge Certification Program, or Sanctioned Competition Program, call or write the American Homebrewers Association, PO Box 1679, Boulder, CO, 80306-1679, (303) 447-0816, FAX (303) 447-2825.

LAGER (con't)	Original Gravity (Balling/Plato)	Percent Alc./Vol.	Int'l Bittering Units	Color SRM
15. Classic Pilsner				
a) German	1.044-50 (11-12.5)	4-5%	30-40	2.5-4
b) Bohemian	1.044-56 (11-14)	4-5%	35-45	3-5
16. American Lager				
a) Diet/Lite	1.024-40 (6-10)	2.9-4.2%	8-15	2-4
b) American Standard	1.040-46 (10-11.5)	3.8-4.5%	5-17	2-4
c) American Premium	1.046-50 (11.5-12.5)	4.3-5%	13-23	2-8
d) Dry	1.040-50 (10-12.5)	4-5%	15-23	2-4
e) Cream Ale/Lager	1.044-55 (11-14)	4.5-7%	10-22	2-4
f) American Dark	1.040-50 (10-12.5)	4-5.5%	14-20	10-20
17. Vienna/Oktoberfest/Märzen				
a) Vienna	1.048-55 (12-13.5)	4.4-6%	22-28	8-12
b) Märzen/Oktoberfest	1.052-64 (13-16)	4.8-6.5%	22-28	7-14

MIXED STYLE (LAGER-ALE)

	Original Gravity (Balling/Plato)	Percent Alc./Vol.	Int'l Bittering Units	Color SRM
18. German Style Ale				
a) Düsseldorf-style Altbier	1.044-48 (11-12)	4.3-5%	25-35	11-19
b) Kölsch	1.042-46 (10.5-11.5)	4.4-5%	20-30	3.5-5
19. Fruit Beer				
a) Fruit Beer	1.030-1.110 (7.5-27.5)	2.5-12%	5-70	5-50
b) Classic-style Fruit Beer	(refer to individual styles)			
20. Herb Beer				
a) Herb Beer	1.030-1.110 (7.5-27.5)	2.5-12%	5-70	5-50
b) Classic-style Herb Beer	(refer to individual styles)			
21. Specialty Beer				
a) Specialty Beer	1.030-1.110 (7.5-27.5)	2.5-12%	0-100	0-100
b) Classic-style Specialty Beer	(refer to individual styles)			
22. Smoked Beer				
a) Bamberg-style Rauchbier	1.048-52 (12-13)	4.3-4.8%	20-30	10-20
b) Classic-style Smoked Beer	(refer to individual styles)			
c) Other	(varies widely)			
23. California Common Beer				
a) California Common Beer	1.040-55 (10-14)	3.6-5%	35-45	8-17
24. Wheat Beer (Ale)				
a) Berliner Weisse	1.028-32 (7-8)	2.8-3.4%	3-6	2-4
b) German-style Weizen/ Weissbier	1.048-56 (12-14)	4.8-5.4%	10-15	3-9
c) German-style Dunkelweizen	1.048-56 (12-14)	4.8-5.4%	10-15	17-22
d) German-style Weizenbock	1.066-80 (16.5-20)	6.5-7.5%	10-20	7-30
25. Traditional Mead				
a) Sparkling	1.050-90 (12.5-22.5)	5-11%	0	0-4
b) Still	1.090-1.140 (22.5-35)	11-15%	0	0-5
26. Melomel, Cyser, Pyment, Braggot				
a) Sparkling	1.050-90 (12.5-22.5)	5-11%	0-15	—
b) Still	1.090-1.140 (22.5-35)	11-15%	0-20	—
27. Metheglin, Hippocras				
a) Sparkling	1.050-90 (12.5-22.5)	5-11%	0-15	—
b) Still	1.090-1.140 (22.5-35)	11-15%	0-20	—
28. Cider				
a) Still	1.045-.053	7%	—	—
b) Sparkling	1.045-.061	8%	—	—
c) New England-style	1.061-1.105	8-14%	—	—
d) Specialty Cider	1.045-1.105	5.8-14%	—	—
29. Saké				
a) Saké (Japanese rice beer)	12-20		—	—
b) Sparkling Saké		12.5%	—	—
c) Other Oriental Rice Beers	varies with style	—	—	

American Homebrewers Association
1994 National Homebrew Competition

BEER SCORE SHEET

The following is the 1994 American Homebrewers Association's beer score sheet. The Beer score sheet is updated annually and used in homebrew competitions. For more information on the National Homebrew Competition, Beer Judge Certification Program, or Sanctioned Competition Program, call or write the American Homebrewers Association, PO Box 1679, Boulder, CO, 80306-1679, (303) 447-0816, FAX (303) 447-2825.

DESCRIPTOR DEFINITIONS
✔ CHECK WHENEVER APPROPRIATE

☐ **Acetaldehyde**—Green applelike aroma; byproduct of fermentation.

☐ **Alcoholic**—The general effect of ethanol and higher alcohols. Tastes warming.

☐ **Astringent**—Drying, puckering (like chewing on a grape skin) feeling often associated with sourness. Tannin. Most often derived from boiling of grains, long mashes, oversparging, or sparging with hard water.

☐ **Bitter**—Basic taste associated with hops, braun-hefe, or malt husks. Sensation experienced on back of tongue.

☐ **Chill haze**—Haze caused by precipitation of protein-tannin compound at cold temperatures. Does not affect flavor. Reduction of proteins or tannins in brewing or fermenting will reduce haze.

☐ **Chlorophenolic**—Caused by chemical combination of chlorine and organics. Detectable in parts per billion. Aroma is unique but similar to plasticlike phenolic. Avoid using chlorinated water.

☐ **Cooked Vegetable/Cabbagelike**—Aroma and flavor often due to long lag times and wort spoilage bacteria that later are killed by alcohol produced in fermentation.

☐ **Diacetyl/Buttery**—Described as buttery, butterscotch. Sometimes caused by abbreviated fermentation or bacteria.

☐ **DMS** (dimethyl sulfide)—A sweet, cornlike aroma/flavor. Can be attributed to malt, short or non-vigorous boiling of wort, slow wort chilling, or, in extreme cases, bacterial infection.

☐ **Fruity/Estery**—Similar to banana, raspberry, pear, apple, or strawberry flavor; may include other fruity/estery flavors. Often accentuated with higher temperature fermentations and certain yeast strains.

☐ **Grainy**—Raw grain flavor. Cereallike. Some amounts are appropriate in some beer styles.

☐ **Hoppy**—Characteristic odor of the essential oil of hops. Does not include hop bitterness.

☐ **Husky**—See Astringent.

☐ **Light-struck**—Having the characteristic smell of a skunk, caused by exposure to light. Some hops can have a very similar character.

☐ **Metallic**—Caused by exposure to metal. Also described as tinny, coins, bloodlike. Check your brewpot and caps.

☐ **Oxidized/Stale**—Develops in the presence of oxygen as beer ages or is exposed to high temperatures; winy, wet cardboard, papery, rotten vegetable/pineapple, sherry, baby diapers. Often coupled with an increase in sour, harsh, and bitter. The more aeration in bottling/siphoning or air in headspace, the more quickly beer will oxidize. Warm temperatures dramatically accelerate oxidation.

☐ **Phenolic**—Can be any one or combination of a medicinal, plastic, electrical fire, Listerinelike, Band-Aidlike, smoky, or clovelike aroma or flavor. Most often caused by wild strains of yeast or bacteria. Can be extracted from grains (see Astringent). Sanitizing residues left in equipment can contribute.

☐ **Salty**—Flavor associated with table salt. Sensation experienced on sides of tongue. Can be caused by presence of too much sodium chloride, calcium chloride or magnesium sulfate (Epsom salts); brewing salts.

☐ **Solvent like**—Flavor and aromatic character of certain alcohols, often due to high fermentation temperatures. Like acetone, lacquer thinner.

☐ **Sour/Acidic**—Pungent aroma, sharpness of taste. Basic taste like vinegar or lemon; tart. Typically associated with lactic or acetic acid. Can be the result of bacterial infection through contamination or the use of citric acid. Sensation experienced on sides of tongue.

☐ **Sweet**—Basic taste associated with sugar. Sensation experienced on front tip of tongue.

☐ **Sulfurlike(H_2S; Hydrogen sulfide)**—Rotten eggs, burning matches. Is a byproduct with certain strains of yeast. Fermentation temperature can be a factor of intensity. Diminishes with age. Most evident with bottle-conditioned beer.

☐ **Yeasty**—Yeastlike flavor. Often due to strains of yeast in suspension or beer sitting on sediment too long.

American Homebrewers Association
1994 National Homebrew Competition

Round No. _____ **Entry No.** _____

Category No. _____

Subcategory (spell out) _____

Judged By (please print) _____

Judge Qualifications (check one)   □ Recognized   □ Certified

□ National   □ Master   □ Experienced (but not in BJCP)

□ Apprentice or Novice   □ Other: _____

BOTTLE INSPECTION Comments _____

_____

	Max. Score
BOUQUET/AROMA (as appropriate for style)	10_____

Malt (3), Hops (3), Other aromatic characteristics (4)

Comments _____

_____

APPEARANCE (as appropriate for style)   6_____

Color (2), Clarity (2), Head retention (2)

Comments _____

_____

FLAVOR (as appropriate for style)_____ 19 _____

Malt (3), Hops (3), Conditioning (2), Aftertaste (3), Balance (4), Other flavor characteristics (4)

Comments _____

_____

BODY (full or thin as appropriate for style)   5 _____

Comments _____

_____

_____

DRINKABILITY & OVERALL IMPRESSION   10 _____

Comments _____

_____

_____

TOTAL (50 possible points):_____

Scoring Guide		
	Excellent (40-50):	Exceptionally exemplifies style, requires little or no attention
	Very Good (30-39):	Exemplifies style well, requires some attention
	Good (25-29):	Exemplifies style satisfactorily, but requires attention
	Drinkable (20-24):	Does not exemplify style, requires attention
	Problem (<20):	Problematic, requires much attention
		Use other side for additional comments. NHC94

American Homebrewers Association
1994 National Homebrew Competition

MEAD SCORE SHEET

The following is the 1994 American Homebrewers Association's mead score sheet. The score sheet is updated annually and used in homebrew competitions. For more information on the National Homebrew Competition, Beer Judge Certification Program, or Sanctioned Competition Program, call or write the American Homebrewers Association, PO Box 1679, Boulder, CO, 80306-1679, (303) 447-0816, FAX (303) 447-2825.

DESCRIPTOR DEFINITIONS

✔ CHECK WHENEVER APPROPRIATE

☐ **Alcoholic**—The general effect of ethanol and higher alcohols. Tastes warming.

☐ **Astringent**—Drying, puckering (like chewing on a grape skin) feeling often associated with sourness. Tannin. Most often derived from boiling grains, long mashes, oversparging, or sparging with hard water.

☐ **Chlorophenolic**—Caused by chemical combination of chlorine and organics. Detectable in parts per billion. Aroma is unique but similar to plasticlike phenolic. Avoid using chlorinated water.

☐ **Clean**—Lacking off-flavors.

☐ **Cyser**—A type of mead made with apple juice.

☐ **Floral**—The aroma of flower blossoms.

☐ **Fruity/Estery**—Similar to banana, raspberry, pear, apple, or strawberry flavor; may include other fruity/estery flavors. Often accentuated with higher temperature fermentations and certain yeast strains.

☐ **Light-struck**—Having the characteristic smell of a skunk, caused by exposure to light. Some hops can have a very similar character.

☐ **Melomel**—A type of mead made with fruit.

☐ **Metallic**—Caused by exposure to metal. Also described as tinny, coins, bloodlike. Check your brewpot and caps.

☐ **Metheglins**—A type of mead made with herbs and/or spices.

☐ **Oxidized/Stale**—Develops in the presence of oxygen as mead ages or is exposed to high temperatures; winy, wet cardboard, papery, rotten vegetable/pineapple, sherry, baby diapers. Often coupled with an increase in sour, harsh, and bitter. The more aeration in bottling/siphoning or air in headspace, the more quickly a mead will oxidize. Warm temperatures dramatically accelerate oxidation.

☐ **Phenolic**—Can be any one or combination of a medicinal, plastic, electrical fire, Listerinelike, Band-Aidlike, smoky, or clovelike aroma or flavor. Most often caused by wild strains of yeast or bacteria. Can be extracted from grains (see astringent). Sanitizing residues left in equipment can contribute.

☐ **Pyment**—A type of mead made with grapes.

☐ **Salty**—Flavor associated with table salt. Sensation experienced on sides of tongue. Can be caused by presence of too much sodium chloride, calcium chloride or magnesium sulfate (Epsom salts); brewing salts.

☐ **Solvent like**—Flavor and aromatic character of certain alcohols, often due to high fermentation temperatures. Like acetone, lacquer thinner.

☐ **Sour/Acidic**—Pungent aroma, sharpness of taste. Basic taste like vinegar or lemon; tart. Typically associated with lactic or acetic acid. Can be the result of bacterial infection through contamination or the use of citric acid. Sensation experienced on sides of tongue.

☐ **Sparkling**—Having carbonation.

☐ **Still**—Lacking carbonation.

☐ **Sweet**—Basic taste associated with sugar. Sensation experienced on front tip of tongue.

☐ **Sulfurlike (H₂S; Hydrogen sulfide)**—Rotten eggs, burning matches. Is a byproduct with certain strains of yeast. Fermentation temperature can be a factor of intensity. Diminishes with age. Most evident with bottle-conditioned mead.

☐ **Traditional Mead**—Honey and water fermented, having no types of flavorings.

☐ **Yeasty**—Yeastlike flavor. Often due to strains of yeast in suspension or mead sitting on sediment too long.

Round No. _____ **Entry No.** _____

Category No. _____

Subcategory (spell out) _____

Judged By (please print) _____

Judge Qualifications (check one) ☐ Recognized ☐ Certified

☐ National ☐ Master ☐ Experienced (but not in BJCP)

☐ Apprentice or Novice ☐ Other: _____

BOTTLE INSPECTION Comments _____

_____

	Max. Score

BOUQUET/AROMA (as appropriate for style) 10 _____

Expression of Honey (5), Expression of other ingredients as appropriate (5)

Comments _____

_____

_____

_____

APPEARANCE (as appropriate for style) 6 _____

Color (3), Clarity (3)

Comments _____

_____

_____

FLAVOR (as appropriate for style)_____ 24 _____

Expression of Honey (5), Balance of: acidity, sweetness, alcohol strength, body, carbonation (if appropriate). and other ingredients as appropriate (14), Aftertaste (5)

Comments _____

_____

_____

DRINKABILITY & OVERALL IMPRESSION 10 _____

Comments _____

_____

_____

TOTAL (50 possible points):_____

Scoring Guide		
Excellent (40-50):	Exceptionally exemplifies style, requires little or no attention	
Very Good (30-39):	Exemplifies style well, requires some attention	
Good (25-29):	Exemplifies style satisfactorily, but requires attention	
Drinkable (20-24):	Does not exemplify style, requires attention	
Problem (<20):	Problematic, requires much attention	
	Use other side for additional comments.	NHC94

American Homebrewers Association
1994 National Homebrew Competition

CIDER SCORE SHEET

The following is the 1994 American Homebrewers Association's cider score sheet. The score sheet is updated annually and used in homebrew competitions. For more information on the National Homebrew Competition, Beer Judge Certification Program, or Sanctioned Competition Program, call or write the American Homebrewers Association, PO Box 1679, Boulder, CO, 80306-1679, (303) 447-0816, FAX (303) 447-2825.

DESCRIPTOR DEFINITIONS

✔ CHECK WHENEVER APPROPRIATE

☐ **Acetic**—A vinegarlike smell and sharp taste, a distinct fault.

☐ **Acidity**—Malic acid is responsible for the freshness, zing in cider.

☐ **Alcoholic**—The general effect of ethanol and higher alcohols. Tastes warming.

☐ **Astringent**—A drying sensation in the mouth similar to chewing on a teabag. Due to excess tannin and acceptable only in a young cider.

☐ **Aftertaste**—The lingering taste in the back of the throat. Ideally long and pleasant.

☐ **Balanced**—No component of the cider overpowers another. An alcoholic cider is balanced by tannin, a sweet cider is balanced by crisp acidity.

☐ **Body**—The "middle" of a mouthful of cider. Good body will feel heavy in the mouth.

☐ **Bouquet**—Also known as the smell, nose, or aroma.

☐ **Carbonation**—A naturally carbonated cider has small beading bubbles. An artificially carbonated cider has large, uniform bubbles.

☐ **Clarity**—The visual aspect of cider. It may be brilliant, clear, slight haze, haze, or cloudy.

☐ **Clean**—Free of apparent off odors or tastes.

☐ **Color**—Pale yellow, light yellow, yellow, golden. Green tinge or orange hues signify potential problems.

☐ **Dry**—A sensation on the tongue that indicates lack of residual sugar. Varies from bone dry to dry, off-dry and semi-dry.

☐ **Fruity**—May be fruity in flavor and not unpleasant, or fruity in bouquet and not unpleasant either. Quite common due to the aromatic quality of the popular Macintosh apple.

☐ **Hot**—A fault due to excess alcohol.

☐ **Light**—Refers to body and is not a negative, as opposed to thin.

☐ **Metallic**—Caused by exposure to metal. Also described as tinny, coins, bloodlike. Check your brewpot and caps.

☐ **Moldy (musty)**—A closed in, sherry/like smell, like damp cardboard. Due to oxidation or rarely to overzealous filtration.

☐ **Mousy**—A disorder due to lactic-acid bacteria. Cider smells and tastes like a rodent's den.

☐ **New England-style Cider**—A strong cider (+8% alc.) made following traditional methods.

☐ **Phenolic**—A plastic like taste/smell caused by some wild yeasts or bacteria.

☐ **Sparkling**—Having carbonation.

☐ **Still**—Lacking carbonation.

☐ **Sulfury**—Smells like burnt matches. Due to high temperature fermentation or excess use of SO_2.

☐ **Sweet**—Basic taste associated with sugar. May be appropriate for style as in a dessert cider.

☐ **Thin**—Lacking body or "stuffing."

☐ **Woody**—A taste or aroma due to an extended length of time in oak or on wood chips.

☐ **Yeasty**—A breadlike aroma due to a cider sitting on its lees for an extended period.

☐ **Young**—A cider with components that have not yet matured into a balanced whole.

American Homebrewers Association
1994 National Homebrew Competition

Round No. _____ **Entry No.** _____

Category No. _____

Subcategory (spell out) _____

Judged By (please print) _____

Judge Qualifications (check one)   ☐ Recognized   ☐ Certified

☐ National   ☐ Master   ☐ Experienced (but not in BJCP)

☐ Apprentice or Novice   ☐ Other: _____

BOTTLE INSPECTION Comments _____

_____

                                                              Max. Score

BOUQUET/AROMA (as appropriate for style)   **10** _____

Expression of ingredients as appropriate

Comments _____

_____

_____

_____

APPEARANCE (as appropriate for style)   **6** _____

Color (3), Clarity (3)

Comments _____

_____

_____

FLAVOR (as appropriate for style) _____ **24** _____

Balance of adicity, sweetness, alcohol strength, and body carbonation (if appropriate) (14).
Other ingredients as appropriate (5), Aftertaste (5)

Comments _____

_____

_____

DRINKABILITY & OVERALL IMPRESSION   **10** _____

Comments _____

_____

_____

                              TOTAL (50 possible points): _____

Scoring Guide	**Excellent (40-50):**	Exceptionally exemplifies style, requires little or no attention
	Very Good (30-39):	Exemplifies style well, requires some attention
	Good (25-29):	Exemplifies style satisfactorily, but requires attention
	Drinkable (20-24):	Does not exemplify style, requires attention
	Problem (<20):	Problematic, requires much attention
		Use other side for additional comments. NHC94

American Homebrewers Association
1994 National Homebrew Competition

SAKÉ/JIU SCORE SHEET

The following is the 1994 American Homebrewers Association's saké score sheet. The score sheet is updated annually and used in homebrew competitions. For more information on the National Homebrew Competition, Beer Judge Certification Program, or Sanctioned Competition Program, call or write the American Homebrewers Association, PO Box 1679, Boulder, CO, 80306-1679, (303) 447-0816, FAX (303) 447-2825.

DESCRIPTOR DEFINITIONS
✔ CHECK WHENEVER APPROPRIATE

☐ **Alcoholic**—The general effect of ethanol and higher alcohols. Tastes warming.

☐ **Amber Jiu**—Chinese style which has been sherrified (made like sherry, dark color, sherry aroma-acetaldehyde), should be clear (also called Huang jiu).

☐ **Asian Homebrew**—Primitive Asian-style jius. All are cloudy, some sweet, some tart, but never clear.

☐ **Astringent**—Drying, puckering (like chewing on a grape skin) feeling often associated with sourness. Tannin.

☐ **Chlorophenolic**—Caused by chemical combination of chlorine and organics. Detectable in parts per billion. Aroma is unique but similar to plasticlike phenolic. Avoid using chlorinated water.

☐ **Clean**—Lacking off-flavors.

☐ **Doburoku**—Japanese version of Asian Homebrew (see above).

☐ **Floral**—The aroma of flower blossoms.

☐ **Fruit Saké**—May be any appropriate color. Should be clear.

☐ **Fruity/Estery**—Similar to banana, raspberry, pear, apple, or strawberry flavor; may include other fruity/estery flavors. Often accentuated with higher temperature fermentations and certain yeast strains.

☐ **Ginjo**—Saké made with highly polished rice, must be very pale and crystal clear (as water) no sediment whatsoever.

☐ **Genshu**—Full strength saké with no water added at yodan, i.e. about 18.5 to 20 percent alcohol by volume. Must be very pale and crystal clear.

☐ **Herbal Saké**—May be any appropriate color. Should be clear.

☐ **Jiu Niong**—Chinese version of Asian Homebrew (see above).

☐ **Koji Nose**—The bouquet of the jiu, as it is affected by the action of the koji (isoamyl acetate).

☐ **Makolee (Mak-joo)**—Korean version of Asian Homebrew (see above).

☐ **Moromi Saké**—A form of Nigori Saké (see below).

☐ **Metallic**—Caused by exposure to metal. Also described as tinny, coins, bloodlike. Check your brewpot and caps.

☐ **Nigori Saké**—Unfiltered, unrefined, cloudy saké. MUST have sediment, and be sampled with sediment in suspension, MUST be opaque or nearly so after being shaken in the bottle. Not clear.

☐ **Oxidized/Stale**—Develops in the presence of oxygen as saké ages or is exposed to high temperatures; winy, wet cardboard, papery, rotten vegetable/pineapple, sherry, baby diapers. Often coupled with an increase in sourness, harshness and bitterness. The more aeration in bottling/siphoning or air in headspace, the more quickly a saké will oxidize. Warm temperatures dramatically accelerate oxidation.

☐ **Phenolic**—Can be any one or combination of a medicinal, plastic, electrical fire, Listerinelike, Band-Aidlike, smoky, or clovelike aroma or flavor. Most often caused by wild strains of yeast or bacteria. Sanitizing residues left in equipment can contribute.

☐ **Solventlike**—Flavor and aromatic character of certain alcohols, often due to high fermentation temperatures. Like acetone, lacquer thinner.

☐ **Sour/Acidic**—Pungent aroma, sharpness of taste. Basic taste like vinegar or lemon; tart. Typically associated with lactic or acetic acid. Can be the result of bacterial infection through contamination or the use of citric acid. Sensation experienced on sides of tongue.

☐ **Sparkling**—Having carbonation.

☐ **Still**—Lacking carbonation.

☐ **Sweet**—Basic taste associated with sugar. Sensation experienced on front tip of tongue.

☐ **Sulfurlike (H₂S; Hydrogen sulfide)**—Rotten eggs, burning matches. Is a byproduct with certain strains of yeast. Fermentation temperature can be a factor of intensity. Diminishes with age. Most evident with bottle-conditioned saké.

☐ **Yeasty**—Yeastlike flavor. Often due to strains of yeast in suspension or saké sitting on sediment too long.

American Homebrewers Association
1994 National Homebrew Competition

Round No. _____ Entry No. _____

Category No._____

Subcategory (spell out) _____

Judged By (please print)_____

Judge Qualifications (check one)   ☐ Recognized   ☐ Certified

☐ National   ☐ Master   ☐ Experienced (but not in BJCP)

☐ Apprentice or Novice   ☐ Other: _____

TYPE OF SAKÉ/JIU (check one or more as apprpriate):

☐ Chinese amber rice beer (Huang-chiu)

☐ Korean saké (Taek Ju and other Jus)

☐ Saké variations from other grains (corn, barley, millet, ect.)

☐ Mirin (cooking) saké

BOTTLE INSPECTION Comments _____

_____

		Max. Score

BOUQUET/AROMA (as appropriate for style)   10_____
Expression of Sake/Koji (5), Expression of other ingredients as appropriate (5)

Comments _____

_____

APPEARANCE (as appropriate for style)   6_____
Color (3), Clarity (3)

Comments _____

_____

FLAVOR (as appropriate for style)_____ 24 _____
expression of Sake/Koji (5), Balance of acidity, sweetness, alcohol strength, body, carbonation (if appropriate), Other ingredients as appropriate (14), Aftertaste (5)

Comments _____

_____

DRINKABILITY & OVERALL IMPRESSION   10 _____

Comments _____

_____

_____

TOTAL (50 possible points):_____

Scoring Guide		
Excellent (40-50):	Exceptionally exemplifies style, requires little or no attention
Very Good (30-39):	Exemplifies style well, requires some attention
Good (25-29):	Exemplifies style satisfactorily, but requires attention
Drinkable (20-24):	Does not exemplify style, requires attention
Problem (<20):	Problematic, requires much attention
	Use other side for additional comments.	NHC94

Victory Beer Recipes   **1994 SAKÉ/JIU SCORE SHEET   203**

GLOSSARY

acetification.	The changes brought about by production of acetic acid, generally as spoilage by aerobic bacteria, but also as mash or kettle pH adjustment.
adjunct.	Any unmalted grain or other fermentable ingredient added to the mash.
aeration.	The action of introducing air to the wort at various stages of the brewing process.
airlock.	(see fermentation lock)
airspace.	(see ullage)
alcohol by volume (v/v).	The percentage of volume of alcohol per volume of beer. To calculate the approximate volumetric alcohol content, subtract the terminal gravity from the original gravity and divide the result by 0.0075. For example: 1.050-1.012 = 0.038; 0.038/0.0075 = 5% v/v.
alcohol by weight (w/v).	The percentage weight of alcohol per volume of beer. To calculate the approx. alcohol content by weight subtract the terminal gravity and mutiply by 105. For example: 1.050-1.0212 = 0.038x105 = 4% (alcohol content/weight).
ale.	1. Historically, an unhopped malt beverage. 2. Now a generic term for hopped beers produced by top fermentation, as opposed to lagers, which are produced by bottom fermentation.
all-extract beer.	A beer made with only malt extract as opposed to one made from barley, or a combination of malt extract and barley.
all-grain beer.	A beer made with only malted barley as opposed to one made from malt extract, or from malt extract and malted barley.
all-malt beer.	A beer made with only barley malt with no adjuncts or refined sugars.
alpha acid.	A soft resin in hop cones. When boiled, alpha acids are converted to iso-alpha-acids, which account for 60 percent of a beer's bitterness.
alpha-acid unit.	A measurement of the potential bitterness of hops, expressed by their percentage of alpha acid. Low = 2 to 4%, medium = 5 to 7%, high = 8 to 12%. Abbrev: A.A.U.
attenuation.	The reduction in the wort's specific gravity caused by the transformation of sugars into alcohol and carbon-dioxide gas.
Balling.	A saccharometer invented by Carl Joseph Napoleon Balling in 1843. It is calibrated for 63.5 degrees F (17.5 degrees C), and graduated in grams per hundred, giving a direct reading of the percentage of extract by weight per 100 grams solution. For example: 10 °B = 10 grams of sugar per 100 grams of wort.
Bitterness Units (BU).	ASBC measurement of bittering substances in beer, primarily iso-

	alpha-acids, but also including oxidized beta acids. Also see International Bitterness Units.
blow-by (blow-off).	A single-stage homebrewing fermentation method in which a plastic tube is fitted into the mouth of a carboy, with the other end submerged in a pail of sterile water. Unwanted residues and carbon dioxide are expelled through the tube, while air is prevented from coming into contact with the fermenting beer, thus avoiding contamination.
carbonation.	The process of introducing carbon-dioxide gas into a liquid by: 1. injecting the finished beer with carbon dioxide; 2. adding young fermenting beer to finished beer for a renewed fermentation (kraeusening); 3. priming (adding sugar) to fermented wort prior to bottling, creating a secondary fermentation in the bottle.
carboy.	A large glass, plastic, or earthenware bottle.
chill haze.	Haziness caused by protein and tannin during the secondary fermentation.
DMS.	Abbrieviation for dimethyl sulfide, a major sulfer compound of lagers. DMS is released during boiling as a gas that dissipates into the atmosphere.
dry hopping.	The addition of hops to the primary fermenter, the secondary fermenter, or to casked beer to add aroma and hop character to the finished beer without adding significant bitterness.
dry malt.	Malt extract in powdered form.
EBC (European Brewery Convention).	(see SRM)
extract.	The amount of dissolved materials in the wort after mashing and lautering malted barley and/or malt adjuncts such as corn and rice.
fermentation lock.	A one-way valve, which allows carbon-dioxide gas to escape from the fermenter while excluding contaminants.
final specific gravity.	The specific gravity of a beer when fermentation is complete.
fining.	The process of adding clarifying agents to beer during secondary fermentation to precipitate suspended matter.
flocculant yeast.	Yeast which forms large colonies and tends to come out of suspension before the end of fermentation.
flocculation.	The behavior of yeast cells joining into masses and settling out toward the end of fermentation.
Homebrew Bittering Units.	A formula invented by the American Homebrewers Association to measure bitterness of beer. Bittering units can easily be calculated by multiplying the percent alpha acid in the hops by the number of ounces. Example: if 1.5 ounces of 10 percent alpha acid hops were used in a five-gallon batch, the total bittering units would be 15.: 1.5 x 10 = 15 HBU per five gallons.
hop pellets.	Finely powdered hop cones compressed into tablets.Hop pellets are 20 to 30 percent more bitter by weight than the same variety in loose form.
hydrometer.	A glass instrument used to measure the specific gravity of liquids as compared to water, consisting of a graduated stem resting on a weighed float.
International Bitterness Units (IBUs).	The EBC measurement of the concentration of iso-alpha-acids in 34milligrams per liter (parts per million) in wort and beer. Also

see Bitterness Units.

isinglass. A gelatinous substance made from the swim bladder of certain fish and added to beer as a fining agent.

kraeusen. (n.)The rocky head of foam which appears on the surface of the wort during fermentation. (v.) To add fermenting wort to fermented beer to induce carbonation through a secondary fermentation.

lager. (n.) A generic term for any bottom-fermented beer. Lager brewing is now the predominant brewing method worldwide except in Britain where top fermented ales dominate. (v.) To store beer at near-zero temperatures in order to precipitate yeast cells and proteins and improve taste.

lauter tun. A vessel in which the mash settles and the grains are removed from the sweet wort through a straining process. It has a false, slotted bottom and spigot.

liquefaction. The process by which alpha-amylase enzymes degrade soluble starch into dextrin.

malt. Barley that has been steeped in water, germinated, then dried in kilns. This process converts insoluble starchs to soluble substances and sugars.

malt extract. A thick syrup or dry powder prepared from malt.

mashing. Mixing crushed malt with water to extract the fermentables, degrade haze-forming proteins, and convert grain starches to fermentable sugars and nonfermentable carbohydrates.

modification. 1. The physical and chemical changes in barley as a result of malting. 2. The degree to which these changes have occured, as determined by the growth of the acrospire.

original gravity. The specific gravity of wort previous to fermentation. A measure of the total amount of dissolved solids in wort.

pH. A measure of acidity or alkalinity of a solution, usually on a scale of one to 14, where seven is neutral.

Plato. A saccharometer that expresses specific gravity as extract weight in a one-hundred-gram solution at 68 degrees F (20 degrees C). A revised, more accurate version of Balling, developed by Dr. Plato.

primary fermentation. The first stage of fermentation, during which most fermentable sugars are converted to ethyl alcohol and carbon dioxide.

priming sugar. A small amount of corn, malt, or cane sugar added to bulk beer prior to racking or at bottling to induce a new fermentation and create carbonation.

racking. The process of transferring beer from one container to another, especially into the final package (bottles, kegs, etc.).

saccharification. The naturally occurring process in which malt starch is converted into fermentable sugars, primarily maltose.

saccharometer. An instrument that determines the sugar concentration of a solution by measuring the specific gravity.

saison. An amber- or copper-colored top-fermented beer from Wallon, Belgium, and France. It has a fruity flavor and an alcohol content of about 4.5% by weight (5.6% by volume).

secondary fermentation. 1. The second, slower stage of fermentation, lasting from a few weeks to many months depending on the type of beer. 2. A fer-

	mentation occuring in bottles or casks and initiated by priming or by adding yeast.
sparging.	Spraying the spent grains in the mash with hot water to retrieve the remaining malt sugar.
specific gravity.	A measure of a substance's density as compared to that of water, which is given the value of 1.000 at 39.2 degrees F (4 degrees C). Specific gravity has no accompanying units, because it is expressed as a ratio.
SRM (Standard Reference Method) and EBC (European Brewery Convention).	Two different analytical methods of describing color developed by comparing color samples. Degrees SRM, approximately equivalent to degrees Lovibond, are used by the ASBC (American Society of Brewing Chemists) while degrees EBC are European units. The following equations show approximate conversions: ($^\circ$EBC) = 2.65 x ($^\circ$Lovibond) - 1.2 ($^\circ$Lovibond) = 0.377 x ($^\circ$EBC) + 0.45
starter.	A batch of fermenting yeast, added to the wort to initiate fermentation.
strike temperature.	The initial temperature of the water when the malted barley is added to it to create the mash.
torrified wheat.	Wheat which has been heated quickly at high temperature, causing it to puff up, which renders it more easily mashed.
trub.	Suspended particles resulting from the precipitation of proteins, hop oils, and tannins during boiling and cooling stages of brewing.
tun.	Any open tank or vessel. More usually applied to a mashing tub, but until the 19th century commonly used in reference to a fermenting vessel.
ullage.	The empty space between a liquid and the top of its container. Also called airspace or headspace.
v/v.	(see alcohol by volume)
w/v.	(see alcohol by weight)
water hardness.	The degree of dissolved minerals in water.
wort.	The mixture that results from mashing the malt and boiling the hops, before it is fermented into beer.

INDEX

Victory Beer Recipes

Victory Beer Recipes

BOOKS for Brewers and Beer Lovers

Order Now ... Your Brew Will Thank You!

These books offered by Brewers Publications are some of the most sought after reference tools for homebrewers and professional brewers alike. Filled with tips, techniques, recipes and history, these books will help you expand your brewing horizons. Let the world's foremost brewers help you as you brew. Whatever your brewing level or interest, Brewers Publications has the information necessary for you to brew the best beer in the world — your beer.

Please send me more free information on the following: (check all that apply)

◇ Merchandise and Book Catalog   ◇ Institute for Brewing Studies
◇ American Homebrewers Association® ◇ Great American Beer Festival®

Ship to:

Name _____

Address _____

City _____ State/Province _____

Zip/Postal Code _____ Country _____

Daytime Phone (   ) _____

Please use the following in conjunction with an order form when ordering books from Brewers Publications.

Payment Method

◇ Check or Money Order Enclosed (Payable to the Association of Brewers)
◇ Visa   ◇ MasterCard

Card Number   _   _   _   Expiration Date _____

Name on Card _____ Signature _____

Brewers Publications, PO Box 1510, Boulder, CO 80306-1510, U.S.A.; (303) 546-6514; FAX (303) 447-2825

VBR

BREWERS PUBLICATIONS ORDER FORM

GENERAL BEER AND BREWING INFORMATION

QTY.	TITLE	STOCK #	PRICE	EXT. PRICE
_____	The Art of Cidermaking..468		9.95	_____
_____	Brewing Mead...461		11.95	_____
_____	Dictionary of Beer and Brewing...............................462		19.95	_____
_____	Evaluating Beer..465		19.95	_____
_____	Great American Beer Cookbook...............................466		24.95	_____
_____	New Brewing Lager Beer...469		14.95	_____
_____	Victory Beer Recipes...467		11.95	_____
_____	Winners Circle...464		11.95	_____

CLASSIC BEER STYLE SERIES

QTY.	TITLE	STOCK #	PRICE	EXT. PRICE
_____	Pale Ale..401		11.95	_____
_____	Continental Pilsener...402		11.95	_____
_____	Lambic...403		11.95	_____
_____	Oktoberfest, Vienna, Märzen....................................404		11.95	_____
_____	Porter...405		11.95	_____
_____	Belgian Ale..406		11.95	_____
_____	German Wheat Beer..407		11.95	_____
_____	Scotch Ale...408		11.95	_____
_____	Bock...409		11.95	_____
_____	Stout..410		11.95	_____

PROFESSIONAL BREWING BOOKS

QTY.	TITLE	STOCK #	PRICE	EXT. PRICE
_____	Brewery Planner..500		80.00	_____
_____	North American Brewers Resource Directory..............506		100.00	_____
_____	Principles of Brewing Science...................................463		29.95	_____

THE BREWERY OPERATIONS SERIES, Transcripts
From National Micro- and Pubbrewers Conferences

QTY.	TITLE	STOCK #	PRICE	EXT. PRICE
_____	Volume 6, 1989 Conference.......................................536		25.95	_____
_____	Volume 7, 1990 Conference.......................................537		25.95	_____
_____	Volume 8, 1991 Conference, Brewing Under Adversity...538		25.95	_____
_____	Volume 9, 1992 Conference, Quality Brewing — Share the Experience..............539		25.95	_____

BEER AND BREWING SERIES, Transcripts
From National Homebrewers Conferences

QTY.	TITLE	STOCK #	PRICE	EXT. PRICE
_____	Volume 8, 1988 Conference.......................................448		21.95	_____
_____	Volume 10, 1990 Conference.....................................450		21.95	_____
_____	Volume 11, 1991 Conference, Brew Free or Die!..........451		21.95	_____
_____	Volume 12, 1992 Conference, Just Brew It!.................452		21.95	_____

SUBTOTAL _____

Call or write for a free Beer Enthusiast catalog today.
• U.S. funds only.
• All Brewers Publications books come with a money-back guarantee.
*Postage & Handling: $4 for the first book ordered, plus $1 for each book thereafter. Canadian and international orders please add $5 for the first book and $2 for each book thereafter. Orders cannot be shipped without appropriate P&H.

Colo. Residents Add
3% Sales Tax _____

P&H * _____

TOTAL _____

Brewers Publications, PO Box 1510, Boulder, CO 80306-1510, U.S.A.; (303) 546-6514; FAX (303) 447-2825

VBR

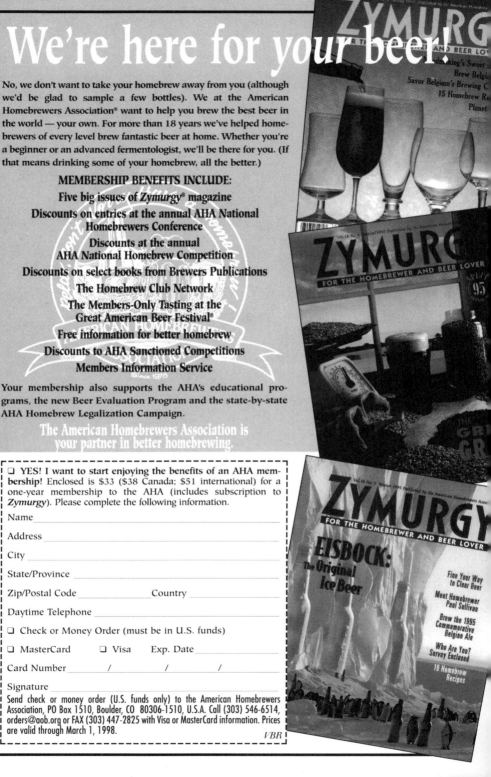

We're here for your beer!

No, we don't want to take your homebrew away from you (although we'd be glad to sample a few bottles). We at the American Homebrewers Association® want to help you brew the best beer in the world — your own. For more than 18 years we've helped homebrewers of every level brew fantastic beer at home. Whether you're a beginner or an advanced fermentologist, we'll be there for you. (If that means drinking some of your homebrew, all the better.)

MEMBERSHIP BENEFITS INCLUDE:

Five big issues of *Zymurgy*® magazine

Discounts on entries at the annual AHA National Homebrewers Conference

Discounts at the annual AHA National Homebrew Competition

Discounts on select books from Brewers Publications

The Homebrew Club Network

The Members-Only Tasting at the Great American Beer Festival®

Free information for better homebrew

Discounts to AHA Sanctioned Competitions

Members Information Service

Your membership also supports the AHA's educational programs, the new Beer Evaluation Program and the state-by-state AHA Homebrew Legalization Campaign.

The American Homebrewers Association is your partner in better homebrewing.

"I read it in *The New Brewer.*"

Jerry Bailey, President,
Old Dominion Brewing Co.,
Ashburn, Va.

Industry leaders like Jerry Bailey know that only *The New Brewer* provides the inside informa-tion craft brewers from coast to coast depend on. Each issue is packed with vital statistics for business planning, the latest in brewing techniques, alternative technologies, beer recipes, legislative alerts, marketing and distribution ideas — everything you need to succeed in today's competitive market.

Whether you're an established brewery or just in the planning stages, our in-depth coverage will give you information you can put to work immediately. After all, your business is our business.

The **New Brewer** • YOUR INSIDER'S VIEW TO THE CRAFT-BREWING INDUSTRY